At Home in the Universe

Gift to the
Church on the Hill
Lending Library
From
Rev. Dr. Dorothea W. Harvey

At Home in the Universe

Re-envisioning the Cosmos with the Heart

JOHN L. HITCHCOCK

Chrysalis Books
West Chester, Pennsylvania

©2001 by John L. Hitchcock

All rights reserved. No part of this publication may be reproduced or transmitted in any form or by any means, electronic or mechanical, including photocopying, recording, or any information storage or retrieval system, without prior permission from the publisher.

Library of Congress Cataloging-in-Publication Data

Hitchcock, John L., 1936–
   At home in the universe : re-envisioning the cosmos with the heart / John L. Hitchcock
   p.   cm.
   Includes bibliographical references and index.
   ISBN 0-87785-396-7 (pbk.)
   1. Religion and science.
   2. Psychology, Religious.
   3. Physics–Religious aspects.
   I. Title.
BL240.2 .H527 2001
215–dc21   2001032596

Edited by Stuart Shotwell
Cover design by Karen Connor
Text design by Sans Serif, Inc., Saline, Michigan
Set in Bodoni by Sans Serif, Inc.
Printed in the United States of America.

Credits:
Original illustrations and figures by Bob Colburn
The poem appearing on page xxviii is from *Year's End*, ©2001 by the Estate of Josephine Johnson Cannon and is printed by permission of the author's estate.
The poem by Rumi appearing on page 3 is from the *Mathnawi*, translated by Coleman Barks in *Delicious Laughter*, and is printed by permission of the translator.
The poems "Pound Floors" (p. 173) and "The Herder" (p. 142) by Sheila Moon are reprinted by permission of the Guild for Psychological Studies Publishng House, San Francisco, California.
Chrysalis Books is an imprint of the Swedenborg Foundation, Inc.
"Anthem for St. Cecilia's Day," copyright 1945 by W. H. Auden (p. xv); "For the Time Being" (p. 63), from *W. H. Auden: Collected Poems* by W. H. Auden, copyright © 1976 by Edward Mendelson, William Meredith, and Monroe K. Spears, Executors of the Estate of W. H. Auden.
Used by permission of Random house, Inc.

For more information, contact:
Swedenborg Foundation Publications
320 North Church Street
West Chester, Pennsylvania 19380
or
http://www.swedenborg.com.

Scientific caution, which does not take into account the human soul's hunger for orientation, tries to appease with stones instead of offering the staff of life. This leads human beings to go wherever they can to find bread, even if it is of the cheapest kind. Since science refutes the human quest for meaning, it drives us to search for it in the collective movements, even though in reality these hollow us out from within or destroy us from without.

—Erich Neumann, *The Place of Creation*

It is only with the heart that one can see rightly; what is essential is invisible to the eye.

—Antoine Saint-Exupéry, *The Little Prince*

To Hermes
divine messenger, lord of mystery

Contents

Chapter titles are qualities inherent in the cosmos.

- ix   Acknowledgments
- xi   Preface
- xv   Prologue: Loving

- 3   Chapter 1: Evolving
- 24   Chapter 2: Self-Creating
- 47   Chapter 3: Unfolding Beauty
- 68   Chapter 4: Godding
- 85   Chapter 5: Awakening
- 102   Chapter 6: Fostering (Cosmic Ecology)
- 117   Chapter 7: Physical Gathering and Layering
- 135   Chapter 8: Psychic Gathering and Layering
- 155   Chapter 9: Integrating
- 173   Chapter 10: Healing

- 186   Appendix 1: Contrast-Knowledge and Field-Knowledge
- 193   Appendix 2: The Cycle of Archaic Identity: The Evolution of Consciousness in the Collective
- 196   Notes
- 204   References
- 208   Index

Acknowledgments

Most of this book was written while I enjoyed the hospitality of Alan and Margie Schedin, my wife's parents, who sustained us while I was awaiting my first employment as a mental-health counselor in 1998, and I thank them deeply. It is an integration of shorter pieces written while I was employed in the physics department of the University of Wisconsin at LaCrosse. I am grateful to have had that opportunity as well. Ros Pickhardt read and critiqued the manuscript prior to submission, and the support and focus that I derive from her friendship is immense. Stuart Shotwell edited the book at all levels, by which I mean not only from submission to production, but also from tiniest details to overall sweep, and as with my previous book, gave unbelievable caring to the project.

My main spiritual support, however, as well as my most profound critic, remains my wife Carrie, for she has the task of informing me that what I hoped would be clear on first writing generally isn't. Her love sustains me always.

Preface

The eighteenth-century seer Emanuel Swedenborg suggested that the cosmos was created so "that there should be a heaven from the human race."[1] The inner movement in this statement is truly profound, especially if we realize that our current idea of "human" may be too limited. In view of our knowledge of biological diversity and of the likelihood of life in the cosmos, Swedenborg's "human" may be extended to any living creature with a consciousness sufficient to be self-aware. Thus, we might say that Swedenborg intuited the purpose of creation in the raising of its creatures to the highest form of consciousness—which he believed was to be found in heaven.

This vision of Swedenborg's projected the fulfillment of the purpose of creation beyond the death of living creatures. He envisioned heavenly societies, charged with the well-being of living humans, and hellish societies that also exerted influence upon the living, so that, in his view, human freedom consists in the equilibrium between the pull of dark and the pull of light upon us. Though Swedenborg saw the cosmos as a good creation that had degenerated—a view contrary to my own belief in the evolution of consciousness and the capacity for love—his view of "angels" as emissaries of a spirit-world finds considerable resonance in the concept of the "field" that will be developed in this book.

My own view is that the purpose of creation is the *fulfillment of love,* an idea that shares quite a bit with its Swedenborgian predecessor. A completely unitary God would have no object to love, so the creation of living creatures makes sense. Yet such creatures, even if they lived in inherent freedom, would be on an unequal footing in the loving relationship with their Creator. Thus, that love would have a fundamental defect and never achieve its true fulfillment, which requires equality on both sides.

The Danish philosopher Søren Kierkegaard struggled with this inequality and came up with a beautiful and justly famous "parable of the king who loved a humble maiden."[2] In the parable, the king was anguished at the inequality of their positions, knowing their love would never really be love; this led him to devise an incognito. Then the maiden could choose the king without giving in to him through awe or from some other motive less lofty. For Kierkegaard, the incognito of God, in wooing humanity, is the Christ. In this case, so much more is at stake than in the case of the king and the maiden that the "disguise" of God must be absolutely seamless: the Christ must be fully human. God had considered the possibility of elevating humanity, but creatures cannot be God. Therefore, God descended to meet humanity on its own ground.

It is true that the fulfillment of love can only occur on a basis of equality. But this book explores another solution to that problem, one called the Godding of humanity. In this process, true consciousness develops out the cosmos, specifically through moral development. In the end, God's need for the fulfillment of love is satisfied as that fulfillment occurs between creatures, as God loving God, but only if the creatures become conscious of themselves and each other as God-centers of consciousness. I need hardly say that this is not yet our usual attitude toward ourselves and others.

I hope to point out, furthermore, that, if we do not know ourselves as centers of God, that means that God does not quite know the God-center, either. Yet how can there be anything that God, the omniscient, does not know? The totality of all spirit and matter in the cosmos does possess what I call omniscience; but, in my definition, omniscience is an *unconscious* patterning. That is, God lacks the kind of consciousness through which love may find fulfillment.

The notion of a God that is not conscious except through us is disturbing and frightening at first. But seeing the cosmos in this way liberates us to understand much that is baffling in our lives, including the presence of suffering. It frees us, too, to love more largely; and it shows us that we are in fact very much at home in this universe, though the cosmos can seem a hostile place.

Much acculturation, conscious and unconscious, blocks our way to this vision of things. Therefore, we need to re-envision the cosmos, this time with the heart.

PROLOGUE

Loving

> O dear white children casual as birds,
> Playing among the ruined languages,
> So small beside the large confusing words,
> So gay against the greater silences
> Of dreadful things you did: O hang the head,
> Impetuous child with the tremendous brain,
> O weep, child, weep, O weep away the stain,
> Weep for the lives your wishes never led.
> . . . .
> O bless the freedom that you never chose.
> . . . .
> O wear your tribulation like a rose.
>
> —W. H. AUDEN, "Anthem for St. Cecilia's Day"

This book is a declaration of love. It is not a declaration of *my* love, but of the fact that love is the heart of the universe. This declaration is not so surprising in relation to the realm of the cosmos that is spirit, for humans have felt since very ancient times that God, as love, is the heart of the universe. However, to claim that the material realm of the cosmos is love as well goes against much that we have been taught.

Yet such is my claim. Love is the weaver, the mediator of all that happens in both realms. In fact, there really is only one realm: spirit-matter, a unity that underlies all that we often experience separately as spirit or as matter. Where we do perceive this unity, we do not perceive it by means of the intellect alone; we apprehend it with the heart as well, which is why we need now to employ the heart in re-envisioning the cosmos.

In this book, I will not attempt to unravel the mystery of love; I can only attempt to say where and how I feel it at work in the universe. Love, as I see it, is creative and freeing, and I will show that the cosmos inherently holds both of these qualities. Since the love of the cosmos is a given (in a sense we will see) and love is binding, it is we who must submit to the bonds of love. And since love sets its object free—since love is the very basis of our freedom—in submitting to its bonds, we also set free whomever or whatever is the object of our love. In a profound sense, which I hope will become clear as we go, our submitting to the bonds of love can help release even God. We can love reality as it is, though it seems to throw obstacles in our way and wound us.

Essayist and novelist Charles Williams expressed this when he said that to love anything but fact is not love.[1] So often we love only our own imagined version of the realities of life and the world. This means also that, in re-envisioning the cosmos with the heart, the facts of the cosmos as known by science must retain their full value. We seek the real in the physical sense as well as the spiritual.

Love does not mean submerging ourselves in feeling. We need not let go of our minds in order to use our hearts. Gains in awareness or consciousness, and in knowledge as well, only increase our capacity to love, no matter what stage we may be evolving through. As we become more conscious, we become more aware of choices; in understanding our choices, we gain freedom of will; and only in freedom is love truly itself. Love cannot be chained. To say this a different way, love is not the subjective feeling of love, however much we love that feeling. Love is something we *do* in relation to the people and things we value. The feeling of love is a by-product of the action of loving. True loving is possible only to the extent that we have developed true *seeing*, for only then do we know what we are doing and choose it freely. This point brings us back to the purpose of this book—which is to attempt to articulate a way of *seeing with the heart*.

I said that the mind need not be sacrificed for this purpose, but the mind must learn that it is not the only organ that matters in the perception of the cosmos. In fact, when the re-envisioning of the cosmos with the heart is complete, the whole basis of envisioning itself will have been transformed. Though we begin with the cosmos as seen with the mind, i.e., with the cosmos as presented by science, in the end, the heart-vision will take its place as the primary vision. We must love—that is the fundamental given of our lives, and that love compels us to seek an ever-truer picture of the physical universe.

The Face of the Cosmos

The universe is not an impersonal process. It has a *face*. It can reflect the radically new as well as the immeasurably old and deep. Wherever we see life, or even the tendency to produce life, we can discern the face of the cosmos. Like the face of an individual, the face of the cosmos is unique. It is no wonder that the cosmos moves toward engendering individuals from the earliest time at which stars and galaxies begin to form, and that the importance of faces and their expressions increases with the complexity of organisms in evolutionary sequence.

The face of the cosmos has many aspects. One is androgynous: a caring face purely integrated from both the maternal and the paternal, though it may seem to be savage and careless.

Another aspect includes the full human range of the feminine, from girl-child to grandmother; another, the similarly complete range of the masculine.

The face of the cosmos is maternal for us because we are its creation; its face might even be called umbilical, connecting our own deepest personal center to that of the cosmos itself, as the source of our own life. It is always present and always accessible to us if we have learned how to look for it.

The face of the cosmos also shows a fatherly aspect. Sometimes it is even a stern father, as reflected in the many myths in which fathers test the courage and skills of their sons. At the least, in any case, it cuts us free, and in that it may seem impersonal. But in spite of our fear that it does not care, we still feel something incredibly personal in it.

The cosmos is in fact both caring *and* freeing, for both of these qualities belong to love.

Perhaps *nature* would be a better word to use than *cosmos;* but when we think of nature, we tend to focus on Earth, with her trees, grasses, rivers, stone, animals, oceans, and weather, and forget the stars and the vast reaches of space. Earth, however, is a part of a whole; and when we examine it in the context of the universe, it shows us that local and distant things are not unlike but the same. Our earth is in fact a window opening onto the whole of nature, and what we see here is repeated in endless variety throughout the cosmos, including life, love, and the search for God.

Science, in its present form, seems to be missing the true face of the cosmos because what it discovers appears to exclude all that is individual and unique. It seeks the most universal and enduring truths it can find concerning matter, not the fleeting and individual facts of our common existence. It insists on repeatable experiments, not unique and individual creations. Yet it is obvious to us all that we live by the creative and the unique, that life thrives on and is built on what is individual. A creatively evolving science must recognize that it does not see the whole. It must learn to see with the heart, as well as with the mind, for there is indeed much more that can be known of the universe and with a deep assurance of its reality. That deep assurance is the province of the seeing heart.

Preparing to See with the Heart

I have spoken of the need for science to see with the heart, but the same is true for each of us. It is time for us to free the heart to participate with the mind in the shaping of consciousness. Over the millennia, the mind has struggled to free itself from the tendrils of emotion, for emotions entangle the seeing of the intellect. It is also true, however, that the mind can darken the vision of the heart, can hold the heart in bondage. Or rather, the repressed emotions express themselves in the blindness and tenacity of rationalism, for their normal functions are undeveloped. What the intellect fails to recognize is that, though the development of the mind tames the wildness of primitive emotions, only a centered *feeling* can prevent the mind from being imprisoned in its life.[2]

Like science, I too have a heart unused to freedom, enchained, as it were, by a life spent in the discipline—the discipline of the old science, science as it has been until now—and from life within social and family structures. Fixed images and mind-sets chain us down without our even knowing it. I who write and you who read must find the freedom that is needed to re-envision the cosmos with the heart and hold ourselves in that freedom as a hummingbird holds itself in the air over a flower.

Whenever we deal with science, we tend to put on a white lab coat, as it were, and assume that what we see with the mind has the ultimate validity. Yet the two greatest physicists of our century, Albert Einstein and Neils Bohr, never lost sight of the heart, and the same has been true of others as well. I for one would measure

PROLOGUE

greatness in scientists by just this standard, for that is what the re-envisioning demands of them.

Freeing ourselves from the chains of our customary attitudes requires permanent vigilance, so great is the power of our attitudes to reassert their imprisonment of our soul. As I write, I too must struggle to remain aware of the qualities that I desire to let through to show forth the heart of the cosmos.

One of the qualities of the cosmos most difficult for me to unchain in myself is play. We use the word *play* in many senses: a set drama, games with rules, self-enjoyment, unseriousness, physical exercise, building sand castles, and trying different ideas out more or less randomly. The cosmos abounds with its own inherent intentionality, which is the other side of play. Indeed, we look deeply into our lives for both of these opposites, intention and play.

Intention insists we go directly to a goal; play suggests we take the roundabout route. However, often we find that the shortest path takes the longest time, and the roundabout path takes the least. A Zen story teaches this:

> Matajuro went to Mount Futara and there found the famous swordsman Banzo. "You wish to study swordsmanship under my guidance?" asked Banzo. "You cannot fulfill the requirements."
>
> "But if I work hard, how many years will it take me to become a master?" persisted the youth.
>
> "The rest of your life," replied Banzo.
>
> "I cannot wait that long," explained Matajuro. "I am willing to pass through any hardship if only you will teach me. If I become your devoted servant, how long might it be?"
>
> "Oh, maybe ten years," Banzo relented.
>
> "My father is getting old, and soon I must take care of him," continued Matajuro. "If I work far more intensively, how long would it take me?"
>
> "Oh, maybe thirty years," said Banzo.

PROLOGUE

> "Why is that?" asked Matajuro. "First you say ten and now thirty years. I will undergo any hardship to master this art in the shortest time."
>
> "Well," said Banzo, "in that case you will have to remain with me for seventy years. A man in such a hurry as you are to get results seldom learns quickly."[3]

Indeed, the story goes on to describe how Banzo began to play with Matajuro, hitting him with a wooden sword when he could, so that Matajuro had to acquire a total mindfulness of everything around him. Thus, through play, he became the greatest swordsman of his time.

Play, in the form of trying things out intuitively, is a large part of problem solving. Even science often finds its way through play, lucky hunches, and the like. The heart also plays: among its healing resources are humor, slips of the tongue, the incongruous. This book will only work with plenty of play. My trained mind rebels; it is impossible, is it not, to "write a book" as pure play? But perhaps I can, with alertness and play, follow a lead other than my own in the gathering of words. I would like the Prime Inhabitant to write it, that deeper part of myself, who was already present in me when I began to awaken from infancy and youth, who both brings me to awakenings and awakens as I do.[4]

For all who seek a truer vision, a vision of the heart, it will help to remember to see this writing as play, a sort of trying out of ways of looking at things. Our understanding changes shapes and costumes time and again—we know that. This is not offered as the final shaping. What is given here is given in joy, like a ball tossed to another in the hope of a game of catch.

Yet, if we could see the world differently, we might live more effectively, and that is a serious matter. The trick is to find the balance between play and seriousness. I know well how counterproductive seriousness can be. For one thing, it can turn people away from what I have to share. It can make people think that I am trying to force them to agree with my way of understanding things. It is true that I have evolved a worldview that seems to me to sum up reality, or else I would not be so bold as to try to share it. But I appreciate that the views of others are often quite as effective for them. So I will try not to insist but merely to present.

As a safeguard, again, I would like to try to stand to one side, so that I may be the recipient of the gift of words, words not my own, words I cannot claim. Ponderous, preaching speech is perhaps the chain of all chains, while light and even speech gives us freedom. Certainly as humans we share a desire to help the world, but the "heavier" we are about it the less likely we are to do any good. Psychologist Erich Neumann used the expression "carefree caring" to describe how we might look at life if we truly entrusted it to the inner guide, the Prime Inhabitant, the Self.[5] The Self is the inner guide not only of the individual, but of humanity as well, and even of all life on Earth. Since the laws of physics are seen to be the same throughout the visible universe, we can assume that psyche and spirit are governed similarly throughout the cosmos. In that case, the Self truly unites everything, though it also accounts for the specificity of each unique being. Pioneer psychologist C. G. Jung described the Self as the archetype of wholeness and totality, which operates both within and without living beings.

By trusting the Self, not only in speech but in all my life, I become light. Heaviness is a lack of that trust. With the lightness I seek, one can pass through pain, and through visions of pain, and still hold to the rightness of the cosmos. I would like to include here what is for me one of the most profound expressions of this lightness, that of Jacques Lusseyran in his autobiography *And There Was Light*.[6]

At eight years of age, Lusseyran was pushed by another boy quite accidentally as they rushed to recess at school. He fell into the corner of a desk and lost both his eyes. Nonetheless, he learned to see inwardly, which included effective orientation in the "outer" world. This is not the place to recapitulate the whole remarkable story, for I only hope to draw on his words to show what I mean by his "lightness." When the Nazis invaded France, Lusseyran was sixteen, but he organized a resistance movement, distributing information on atrocities. Eventually, he was betrayed, arrested, and sent to Buchenwald.

When Lusseyran learned that his best friend had been killed, he was overtaken by a cascade of illnesses. In Buchenwald there were no medicines for prisoners (only a place where the ill were placed until they recovered or died). Dysentery followed pleurisy, and to these were added ear infections and a condition in which his face became "a swollen pulp."

Gradually Lusseyran's body was shutting down; but, at the same time, he began to be filled with a deep sense of aliveness. As he began to let this aliveness take over, he lost all fear. Later he expressed this change by saying that sickness had rescued him from death. He felt life as a powerful substantial thing both within himself and surrounding him:

> I was quite unable to help myself. All of us are incapable of helping ourselves. Now I knew that it was true of the SS among the first. That was something to make one smile.

After several months in the "hospital," Lusseyran, though completely emaciated, had recovered and was able to walk back to his barracks. He was filled with joy and began to help others to learn to live and survive. The other prisoners stopped stealing his food, which had been easy to do because of his blindness.

Lusseyran ends his description of Buchenwald with the older men. Those who had not brought good hearts with them died, most of them in their fifties or sixties. Virtually all of those who survived had good hearts.

> As for them, they were no longer there. They were looking at the world, with Buchenwald in the middle of it, from further away. They absorbed Buchenwald as part of the great outpouring of the universe, but already they seemed to belong to a better world. I found nothing but gladness in the men over seventy.[7]

Lusseyran became light and free not only through his sickness, but through his acceptance of the deep darkness of reality, even to the point that he realized that Hitler's SS troops were "helpless." As he notes, others found this lightness as well.

I wanted to let Lusseyran speak here because he encountered far deeper evil than most of us can imagine. I do not wish to take lightly any of the abundant daily suffering in our wounded world. I am deeply aware of the human betrayal of humanity that surrounds us seemingly without end or mitigation, usually for the sake of someone's profit. Let me say simply that Lusseyran's response to evil stirs something very deep in me. Though it seems an unfathomable mystery that healing has no meaning without the wound and that those most severely tested gain the greatest depth, the heart can find something like a reason if it understands the freedom offered us by the loving universe.

Re-envisioning the Cosmos with the Heart

Hard science, the epitome of seeing the cosmos with the intellect, deletes *life, consciousness, meaning, freedom,* and *love* from its equations. The simplest statement of what it means to re-envision the cosmos with the heart is simply to see the universe in terms of these five. Of course, they form a web with one another as well. Life, love, and freedom, in their more profound meanings, are each essential to the others. Meaning and consciousness are also things of the heart because the heart finds satisfaction through them. This is not to say the intellect does not find satisfaction in meaning and consciousness too, but even the expression "satisfying the mind" links the mind with the heart. The re-envisioning, then, is the *process of discovering these qualities* not only as inherent in the cosmos but also as movers and shapers of what occurs in it. Each of the chapters of this book will bring out some essential aspect of the cosmos and link it back to these five quintessential qualities. The aspects the chapters will explore are evolution, ecology (outer wholeness), creativity, beauty, manifesting the divine, gathering (inclusiveness and the ubiquitous center), and integration (inner wholeness).

Humans always seek to find a deeper basis for things as they are, to come up with a something "behind" it all. It hardly matters what that something is called, for here we struggle with our own wondering. If something, and not nothing, is behind it all, we can ask questions about it and see how the questions make us *feel*. Was the creation, or coming to be, of the cosmos an act of play? Poets have said so. Was it created, or did it come to be from some cosmic need? Is the cosmos not, rather, a gift? These words are a partial response of my own:

THE GIFT
The Gift is the Cosmos—is God
The Gift is Life—is God
The Gift is the Self—is God
The Gift is the Abyss—is God
The Gift is Seeing—completing God,
God's sacrifice of otherness
    for the sake of living—
For only unknowing is alive.

The Gift is another—rooted in God,
  for the sake of loving—
For only finitude makes another possible.
The Gift is Presence—
  majesty, glory, joy, wisdom—
  is God.

God's giving of God's self is a death and rebirth for God, the model of the process that we too must undergo in order to live. For God, it is a dying to eternity and an awakening in time. How can we see this with our heart as God's heart, in which we can participate? Love begets freedom in carefree caring, and freedom in turn begets love. Freedom as a gift also means forgiveness, for when we exercise freedom, we find ourselves as trespassers and wounders of others. We must continually renew our freedom by finding forgiveness, or release, and embody love in granting it. A model for this release is given by Jacques Lusseyran in forgiving his oppressors at Buchenwald—in forgiving indeed the whole of creation for the nature of its wild "outpouring." The need to find and grant forgiveness continually is one of *the problems the universe sets for us that only love can solve.* The cosmos is, in a very real way, a field of love, even if realizing that love costs great pain and suffering.

For me, as I believe for any of us, the experience of hurting others, coupled with the experience of forgiveness, is the thread that holds consciousness and sanity together. The hurting poses the problem, and those whom we have hurt can either invoke self-justification and maintain a distance, or they can invoke love and reestablish the relationship. And, of course, when we are hurt we have the same options, as we know from having to face those inevitable wounds that the highest intentions and efforts cannot avoid.

Awakening to the cosmos does not mean that suddenly all is beauty. We do not suddenly find ourselves bathed in the light of an eternal garden. What about the world's suffering? Do we ignore it because its magnitude is incomprehensible? Rather, we only truly *know* suffering if we share the suffering of "any one person anywhere," in the words of poet Kenneth Patchen.[8]

Franz Werfel was another who fled the Nazism that flooded Germany and greater Europe. At Lourdes, which was only a temporary refuge, he made a vow that, if he escaped, he would write to the glory of the Queen of Heaven. This vow led to his best-known book *The Song of Bernadette*.[9] Then, feeling a further debt to God, he set out to pay it by turning his formidable eloquence to express the suffering of the Holocaust. He had gathered paper, found just the right pen, and had written "Chapter One" at the top when he had an overwhelming vision. Out of that vision, he composed his greatest work, *Star of the Unborn*.[10] A heart attack a few months later confirmed for him the relevance and urgency of the vision. With a doctor at his side, he used the gift of a brief extension of life to give that vision to us. Though others have honored the suffering of the victims of the Nazis, only Werfel could have given us his cosmic vision.

I mention Werfel's story here because *Star of the Unborn* stands behind the present book as a re-envisioning of the cosmos with the heart. It is a magnificent example of the serious play of the cosmos.

We very much need the re-envisioning of the cosmos with the heart. It will help us not just to develop a better "intellectual model" of the cosmos (although it will contribute there as well) but to live fuller lives from the heart. To see truly is to become engaged with life, which again means more effective living. It is much like touring the depressed places of your own city—but not for shock value and not to "get involved with" social issues and problems out of a sense of guilt. The depressed areas of our cities are not "out there" but in ourselves. The environment within us is not depressed because others suffer; it is depressed because we ourselves suffer without understanding. Many years ago, Josephine Johnson wrote:

> Write this on all the pencil-tablets of the mind.
> Write this on all the blackboards of the heart. . . .
> > There shall be no Kingdom and no Commonwealth.
> > There shall be no classless state, and no abundant life,
> > And there shall be no peace—
> > Until each of us, each of us,—squirming here in the too-small desk,
> > In the too-hot room,
> > —Until each of us shall have said,
> > "It is I, Lord. It is I!"[11]

The cosmos will not be re-envisioned with the heart except as each of us undertakes to do so—alone if need be.

Opening our hearts will unveil a reality fuller than the one we have known. And because we have not known it, we have lived less fully than we might if we could really see what is and become a part of it.

We may find again the same facts that science has uncovered concerning the cosmos, but we will find they have new meaning. The paradoxical notions of a cosmos of serious play, of carefree caring, and of finding our weight through lightness, if they can be felt with the heart, can inform us newly as to who we really are. We know these paradoxes in our hearts because they come from the heart of the universe.

At Home in the Universe

CHAPTER I

Evolving

*This loving is also part of infinite Love
without which the world does not evolve.
Objects move from inorganic to vegetation
to selves endowed with spirit through the urgency
of every love that wants to come to perfection.*

—RUMI, Mathnawi

Consciousness is phylogenetically and ontogenetically a secondary phenomenon. It is time this obvious fact were grasped at last.

—C. G. JUNG, Memories, Dreams, Reflections

The transition from seeing the universe with the mind to seeing it with the heart must be grounded in insights that derive from physical facts. Even though in the end the heart-vision is the primary vision for our living, the mind-vision comes first. Without discernment and acceptance of facts, we have only a very partial access to the essential mystery of being, which is far more profound than can be seen with the unaided senses or even with our freest imagination and most profound inspiration. Thus, in order to deepen the seeing of the heart, we must ever return to science, to the mind-vision, for new clues as to the nature of things. Only in that way can we love what truly is. The more sure our vision of physical reality, the more we can see what is behind it as well, and the more we can see the unity of matter and spirit.

If we are to look at an evolving cosmos with the heart as well as the head, then it will be necessary to open the door to some emotional issues that have come to be interwoven with the idea of evolution. Hidden within the concept of evolution, as in an unpleasant cellar, are ideas that we avoid exploring as much as we can. Malleability and openness will be required of our hearts, as we touch upon such issues as the following. How must adjust our understanding of the nature of our awareness, if we decided that consciousness arose from unconscious material? How will our ideas of the survival of the soul or spirit after physical death be affected? And will accepting an evolving cosmos have an impact on how we conceive of God? In the end, will our heart wish to turn away from what we have always seen as fact? Because we firmly resist changes in our worldview, it may not be easy for the heart to accept a new vision.

How can we let ourselves *feel* the cosmos, when we are brought up in a world already loaded with intellectual concepts? If we look again at Jacques Lusseyran's re-envisioning of the world by means of his illness and recovery in the context of war and Nazi attitudes, the sense of re-envisioning with the heart will be a little more clear. The world is not supposed to contain such horrors as the atrocities of those camps. But the fact is that it does. The old men accepted Buchenwald "as part of the great outpouring of the universe." It is not that I want to focus mainly on evil and darkness, but rather that we need to be clear that the acceptance of the reality of darkness can be a herculean labor. On the other hand, it is often equally difficult to accept the greatness of love, which is also part of the "great outpouring." No matter whether we are considering evil or love, the facts are more potent than we are readily willing to accept.

The idea of an evolving cosmos stands either outside of the understanding of many people or in actual opposition to their worldview because the assumption of a static, completed world pervades so many of our cultural institutions. It is, as it were, second nature to us to think that the cosmos has been in some sense "created," that is, "finished"; but the notion of a static cosmos is no more than a blind substitute for a deeper understanding of the underlying reality of things. In religious matters, it shows itself as the image of humanity as a special creation separate from what preceded it; in philosophy, it appears in unconscious assumptions as to the nature of perception; and in physics, it is the refusal to provide for the inclusion of consciousness and meaning in the roots of physical theory.

In order to take the idea of an evolving cosmos seriously, we need to grasp some insights about the nature of being that are inherent in such a cosmos, and we need to incorporate them into our living. The foremost of these insights is the one stated by Jung in the epigraph to this chapter—namely, that consciousness is new to the cosmos. In order even to see this fact, it is necessary to let go of the notion that humans were a special creation placed upon a completed Earth. But one does not simply let go of those notions that one took in preconsciously as a child or that one has assimilated as a matter of faith. It requires a certain strength of conviction, based on repetitive learning, to take as a truthful guide what one truly sees. Jesus of Nazareth said, "If you have ears to hear, then hear," warning that what he was saying would be difficult to take in; it requires an open heart.[1] Our preconceptions cloud our seeing.

It is difficult to put this in exactly the right way. The difficulty lies in the very nature of consciousness. If one is unable to see something that is there, one is at the same time unable to see that one cannot see. We often do not realize that we are only accepting what we have been told, rather than seeing for ourselves. This is because the assimilation of cultural ideas is accompanied by the "aha" feeling, and it all seems to fit together into a whole worldview, which therefore "must be right." Only by means of the long and difficult learning process that engenders consciousness can we learn to honor our own ignorance. We might even say that the hallmark of consciousness is the awareness of one's blindnesses.

But no one *sees* in an ultimate sense. Because of this, the expression "really see" remains relative, a matter of judgment. In some respects the practice of science can help, for one may often be certain of facts; but as noted in the prologue, science itself fails to see the operation of love in the cosmos, which is indeed present there. The very freedom not to see is an aspect of the operation of love in the depths of being.

In his book *Memories, Dreams, Reflections,* Jung puts this latter notion in a way that also permits us to feel his pain at decades of misunderstanding:

> *I realized that one gets nowhere unless one talks to people about the things they know. The naïve person does not appreciate what an insult it is to talk to one's fellow about anything that is unknown to them. They pardon such ruthless behavior only in a writer, journalist, or poet. I came to see that a new idea, or even an unusual aspect of an old one, can be communicated only by facts. Facts remain and cannot be brushed aside; sooner or later someone will come upon them and know what has been found.*[2]

This is the standpoint from which this book is written. The physical facts are solid facts. It is only that we have not followed out their consequences because certain unconscious assumptions still hold sway in the mainstream world. We will now explore some of those facts.

The Evolution of Cosmos and Psyche

Here we will feel our way into a number of aspects of an evolving cosmos. Some of these are central facts, and some are consequences of the central facts. I will be presenting eight of them as numbered items, beginning with physical evolution. The psychic parallels will soon be woven in. While these eight items are not the same as an outline of the book, they introduce many themes still to follow.

> 1. *The cosmos is in a fundamental and permanent state of disequilibrium. Neither it nor its primary constituents can come to a state of permanent rest. There is always some form of imbalance or list (lean, tilt) to the processes that are involved.*

One of the best ways of visualizing this state is to picture the condition of a typical star. It consists of a globe of gases held together by the common gravitational attraction of the atoms of those gases. Since gravity *only* attracts, whereas other physical forces can both attract and repel, if there were no force opposing the contraction of the star, it would collapse to an infinitesimal point. During the major portion of the lifetime of most stars, the main source of the internal pressure that opposes collapse is due to the high temperatures inside the star. Things that are heated build up pressure inside, as can be seen in the case of ordinary pressure cookers.[3] In order to maintain the internal pressure, there must be a continual release of energy within the star. Most of the energy released inside ordinary stars comes from nuclear fusion, converting hydrogen to helium, helium to carbon, and carbon and helium to heavier elements.

The fact that these elements build from the simple to the complex is another major model for evolution as a whole. That building process continues into the complexities of organic and spiritual living, as even the thirteenth-century Sufi poet Rumi knew (see the epigraph).

The star is hot, and to be hot is to radiate energy. If you picture a red-hot piece of iron or the white-hot filament of an incandescent light bulb, you may recall experiencing the heat, the energy given off by the hot iron or the bulb. Hot things radiate energy. It is precisely this inevitable loss of energy that creates the fundamental imbalance of the "being" of the star. Since the star "leaks" off energy as starshine, it must find more internal energy sources, or it will gradually cool; and when it cools, it will shrink since the cooling decreases the internal pressure. But the energy supply of nuclear fuel is finite. It cannot go on indefinitely. Therefore, the star can never be in any permanent equilibrium but will continue to evolve.

The theme of "fundamental disequilibrium" in the cosmos will come up many times in this book, for we too are in permanent disequilibrium. Physicist Ilya Prigogine describes life itself as a "far from equilibrium" process.[4] Just as hot stars radiate energy, so do we. As the stars develop energy internally and dissipate it to their surroundings, so do we, speaking physically, for we also are "hot" relative to the cosmic background.[5]

One difference between living organic beings and stars is that the stars are given their lifetime supply of "fuel" at the time of their formation, while we and all other living forms must "find" the sources of energy in food outside ourselves, which often leads us into conflict with our fellows, both globally and locally. The same is true at the level of psyche and spirit: we must seek that which nourishes us in these dimensions of our being. To go on living, and to evolve, we must move ever further from an equilibrium state. To us, that feels like foregoing "safety." We must learn to handle more and more energy, in transformative stages that begin at conception. But seeking *spiritual* nourishment need not bring us into conflict with other life-forms, which is a wonderful aspect of transformative living in the spiritual dimension of being. We need not enter conflict with others unless, of course, we decide that we need to force-feed others spiritually!

> 2. *The source of energy in the cosmos is* gathering. *The process of gathering and energy release takes many concrete forms. That it is the sole source of physical energy is well known to physicists: whenever any of the four physical forces, namely the strong nuclear force, the weak nuclear force, the electromagnetic force, or the gravitational force are* permitted by circumstances to act to move matter, *energy is released. Usually the force is attracting things to move closer together. For instance, a large boulder may be at rest on a mountainside, but if the circumstances change so as to permit it to roll, the boulder is "gathered" closer to the center of Earth, and energy is released in the process, which might break a tree or blast open a building.*

Only one of these forces, the weakest—namely, gravity—is purely attractive and thus universally releases energy in gathering, bringing matter closer together into more compact forms. But this force dominates the overall processes of the cosmos because the others, being both attractive and repulsive, neutralize themselves overall. Nonetheless, they have important attractive functions, the most significant of which are the building of atomic nuclei and the attraction of electrons to these nuclei to make up ordinary matter.

Since all energy release is explained on the basis of this model of gathering, I call it the "prime law of physics" for convenient reference. At the moment, we will merely introduce this idea. It will be a major theme in chapters 6 and 7.

The psychic equivalent of physical gathering is the gathering of psyche and consciousness into "more compact" forms. One way of gathering contents to our psyche is by means of ordinary "learning" processes, which do indeed strengthen us as persons. Learning is easier if it is not blocked by emotions surrounding traumatic events or by those emotions that protect cultural and family teachings taken in preconsciously or through learning in childhood.

There is another kind of psychic gathering as well. In psychological terms this is the "recollection," or bringing home, of projected contents. However, the applicability of this process goes far beyond the usual conception of projection, which is that we see in others what is in fact inside ourselves, especially our "dark" and "bright" potentials as persons. Again, the usual view is that we get angry when we see another human being exhibiting some quality that we have repressed in ourselves. An especially good example is when we see someone exhibiting some sort of freedom or disorderliness, when we would like to be as free ourselves but simply do not permit ourselves to expand our own boundaries. It is as though the other is "letting the cat out of the bag." The content is something we do not want to admit to ourselves is a personal tendency, and yet there it is, visible for all to see. The measure of the importance of the projection is the amount of gratuitous emotion that surges through us. When we feel the strength of that emotion, we know that there is something for which we need to examine ourselves.

Beyond this usual conception of projection, we also project our own "reality" onto the environment. We feel that we know "how and what things actually are," whether in small matters or great ones, and can hardly be shown, even through facts, that the case is otherwise. Most of us can think of examples regarding others, where we felt that they lacked a clear image of reality because they thought a given situation was something other than we thought it was. But it is the actual structure of the cosmos that is objective (even if it is beyond direct perception), not our opinion regarding that structure. To the extent that we can permit it to do so, that cosmic reality can transform us, which is the same as saying that we can *internalize* the universe. *In principle, there is nothing outside the psyche that does not have its counterpart within.*

We can become one with the universe to the extent that our present inwardly held worldview can be transformed to better fit reality. This can never be a completed process because our capacity to assimilate the cosmos is quite meager at this stage of evolution. I believe that it will always be so; that the universe has infinite depths, so that the highly evolved beings of a billion years hence will also have an infinite way to go toward a complete understanding of the cosmos. This open-ended process will be discussed later at greater length, but it may suffice for now to say that the experience of the mystic vision of union with the cosmos has its source in the ultimate unity of inner and outer.

In view of this, I want to emphasize, here and throughout this book, that the common conception of projection as merely a defense mechanism is very incomplete. By discovering discrepancies between our automatic assumptions (projections) as to what things are like outside ourselves, we gain *self-knowledge* while at the same time we increasingly internalize the universe. Projection is therefore one of the most profound aids to self-discovery. It is only when we "hang on" to a projection that it is seen as a defense. Moreover, projections are the prime means that nature has to bring people together. We would hardly fall in love without them, though we might visualize a future era in which we would be introduced to love in a different manner.

> 3. *The conditions for ego-consciousness were not present in the early stages of cosmic evolution. Consciousness, as we know it, requires an organic being with a brain.*

The capacity for consciousness arises as evolution proceeds to shape the life upon Earth. This is validated by the uniformity of life, shown in the fact that deoxyribonucleic acid (DNA) is its universal basis, along with the fact that we can see the continuity in the evolutionary growth culminating (so far) in the complexity of human DNA. (The question of a divine transcendent consciousness, that is, the question of *God's* consciousness, presents special difficulties, including moral ones. I will return to that question later.)

The first astronomical fact we will use concerning the evolution of the cosmos is the observation of the "primeval fireball," or cosmic background radiation. That is, we observe that our space is filled with certain microwaves, which are the remnant of the explosion, or "Big Bang," with which our cosmos came into existence. This is not the place to deal with the fireball of the Big Bang in detail; but from studying the nature of the fireball radiation and combining that information with what we know of the rate of expansion of the whole cosmos, we conclude that the cosmos originated around fifteen billion years ago as an intense burst of energy, out of which came the forms of matter that we see (or infer) in cosmic space. We have known for over sixty years that the cosmos is expanding. Now we know that, in expanding, it has cooled from a temperature far higher than that in the centers of the hottest stars. The background radiation documents the "flash" of creation, in a particular stage of its cooling.

It is convenient to speak of the cosmos as having evolved from pure hydrogen. This refers to the state of the cosmos when it is between one second and one minute old. We do not have a description of the ultimate first instant of the explosion. The observed fireball radiation reflects the state of the Big Bang flash at the start of the present era, the "matter era." Fuller descriptions of this era and those previous are available in Steven Weinberg's *The First Three Minutes* and Stephen Hawking's *A Brief History of Time*.[6] I mention this moment in which the cosmos was pure hydrogen because the evolution of consciousness requires an organic foundation, which clearly was not present at that time. It had to wait for life to take form on planets, of which there was none until the cosmos was at least one or two billion years old.

Interlude: Surviving Physical Death

One of the great human projections has been that of endowing a future life (a life after death) with the life qualities that we wish we were living here and now. Of course, we can live them now if we are daring enough. Assuming that this issue is on some readers' minds, for it certainly is closely related to the question of consciousness in the universe, we must find a moment in which to speak of it.

Since consciousness, as we know it, is related to the functioning of a physical organism, the question arises as to whether the consciousness of an organic being is now able, or is nearing a time when it might be able, to persist after the physical dissolution of the body in which it developed. This is a critical issue in accepting evolution into our worldview.

We have some evidence from near-death experiences that encourage us, but we have no definite proof. If by "death" we mean a *final* separation of the psyche from a possibility of reconnection with the physical body, then the subjects who reported these experiences had not died at the time they underwent them, though some had been declared dead by attending physicians at the time. Thus, of subjects *returning* from death there remains no proof. Many people dream of the dead in meaningful ways and also sometimes seem to obtain information that they had not known, but our conscious part is generally unaware of what is known in the unconscious, and its impressions are far from definitive proof.

To anticipate a later point, if some beings persist in a personal manner after "death," this persistence must have become possible at some point in the evolution of life on a given planet, when the personal soul became sufficiently coherent. We would otherwise have to (and some do) attribute the persistence of souls to viruses, bacteria, algae, amoebas, trilobites, grasses, trees, ants, or squirrels after the death of their organic physical forms. But life has no definitive beginning in the cosmos; the fundamental aliveness of the cosmos itself comes to actuality by degrees. That tendency to evolve toward more complex forms and fuller being is present in the simplest single atoms.

It seems more probable, then, that there would have to be a threshold condition for survival beyond death, and some individual member of some species would be the first to experience such survival, a being who is alone in the beyond until joined by a similarly successful soul. We do not usually feel that there is such a thing as the soul, or postdeath spirit, of a virus, an amoeba, or a blade of grass, though as I said, some people do indeed prefer this option, and I do feel that the option is open, if we include the souls of atoms, too. It is also possible that beings at our own level maintain coherence for a time after death, though perhaps not permanently, as is usual in the common idea of survival.

What can the heart see or feel with regard to this? Without concrete living, with all its problems, can there be any change or growth in individual lives? This is a heart problem of the first magnitude. If we take ourselves with cosmic lightness, does our state beyond death matter? Are we not here to live and love while we can? If it is right, as I feel, that we give our physical stuff back for the sake of ongoing life on the planet and if our progeny will achieve greater consciousness than ours, does the survival of our souls have any meaning?

Some believe that we survive beyond death in order to help the living. Are we guided by the souls of the tree shrews who evolved into humans in the past sixty-five million years? Could we hope to be of use to our distant offspring, who will be more evolved than we are? Can we even consider these questions with any depth of feeling? Jung once had a dream in which his dead father came to him for marital advice. That is the direction of flow of information (from the living to the dead) that makes most sense to me.

When we consider survival as an achievement based on the evolution of complex forms, we can see how our culture has shaped our concepts. In turn, we can see how drastic a re-envisioning can be, and how difficult.

Unlimited Depth: The Patterning

If life is a "far from equilibrium" process, and the cosmos is in fundamental disequilibrium, is this the same as saying, with the Jesuit paleontologist Teilhard de Chardin, "the universe is fundamentally and primarily living"?[7] This question does not have an easy answer. Needless to say, in a book of this title, the question will be at center stage a lot of the time. If we accept the unity of spirit-matter, and the operation of love, we are already leaning toward a "yes."

> 4. *If the fundamental disequilibrium of the cosmos is an inherent property and continually evolving in such a manner as to manifest more and more of the potentials of the cosmos, it would follow that the cosmos is fundamentally and permanently incomplete. That is, it is eternally in process, or continually and radically unfolding, since there is no way of defining "complete" under the circumstances. If there is also freedom as to what can happen, it follows that there is no conscious knowledge anywhere of what the final goal of the cosmos might be, perhaps not even in God.*

It may be that the goal is the ultimate manifestation of freedom itself, and the creation of beings that live love in a creative manner, continually exploring greater and greater depth in the eternal now. That is, if we take away any fixed or detailed ultimate goal of evolution, we are left free to concentrate on fulfillment in the present life and moment.

Now we are working on the implications of the physical facts given in the first three points.

An immediate corollary of this point is that "ancient wisdom" is not a sole or lone guide for the evolution of consciousness, that our present state is *not* a deterioration from a "golden age." This, of course, flies in the face of our feeling that things are getting worse rather than better, but that only means that we have not known what to expect of evolution. I feel that things are becoming more profound in their implications and that they are getting both worse and better. While it is true that problems are compounding, our capacity to work with them grows as well. This condition requires us to rethink our whole relationship to the "problem" of the origin of evil.

All the long evolutionary while, something is present that represents a complete, or whole, universe and gives us the deep intuition that there is a goal toward which we are moving. Again, if that goal is wholeness, freedom, and creativity, it cannot be fixed or known in advance what forms will emerge in the process.

I feel that we do indeed have guidance in growth, both personally and as a living planet. This comes from the Patterning, which shapes the whole evolution of life. "The Patterning" is what I call that which we attempt to describe with our "laws of physics," but which is ultimately beyond representation.[8] The Patterning also includes the face in the cosmos of which I spoke in the prologue, but I am putting off dealing with whether the Patterning is itself conscious. The Patterning seems to desire (because it is in the process of begetting them) conscious individuals who can receive insight and help the integration of cultures into a whole planetary being. This idea will be developed in chapters 4 and 5.

I believe that this "presence" of the potential wholeness of the cosmos is what gives us our deep (although mistaken) sense that an "answer" was known somewhere all along or that conscious spirits are guiding us in the way things "ought" to go. In that sense, "ancient wisdom," an intuition of ultimate reality, is with us to help us with present problems of living. What is clear, again, is that consciousness has arisen in time and is new and growing.

All of the potentials of the cosmos have been there from the beginning and are in a sense "waiting" for discovery or for actualization. Because we can dimly feel some of them, we sense the greatness of the future just as we do the greatness of the past. The presence of these potentials does not, however, enable us to predict what the next developments will be for any distance into the future.

Is this not the heart's true desire, that God should place us in a universe of infinite depth, which will never run out of creative possibilities? Is it our deepest and best "self" that desires permanent rest from our "labors?" While each of us has a true heart's desire within which we can be fulfilled in our own lives, we do not really want a limit on the depth toward which the planet and the cosmos as a whole can evolve.

Consider that, on a planet less than five billion years old, consciousness has begun to show within the last two million years and that our sun has left to it another five-to-six billion years of its main lifetime. In light of these facts, the human potential to promote and achieve consciousness (as well as the potential to understand the darkness within creation) can be seen to be enormous. At the same time, it is natural to project our intuitive sense of the possible evolutionary developments of the future backward onto the past and see our system as running down from a Golden Age, when life was perfect, toward an age of iron and clay. This feeling can be accounted for in terms of the loss of primordial innocence that a growing consciousness entails. However, a truly growing consciousness is forever innocent, for it is open and opening, however much pain and suffering it has seen. It is aware of its ongoing unfolding and can still play in freedom. As the artist Marc Chagall said, "A pure spirit remains pure in whatever it does."[9]

> 5. *The presence of all of the potentials of the cosmos is indeed the Patterning. Since the realization of some of these potentials precludes the realization of others, we cannot tell which way things must go. Thus, what is in fact actualized at present shapes the future because each concrete choice excludes the option that was not chosen.*

A universe that includes choice must therefore have an open and undetermined future. That is freedom. If a given option is taken, the choices in the future will follow upon that condition, rather than on another that might have been taken.[10] What remains to be known is always infinite in relation to what is known at present.

The nature and importance of choice in the universe is the result of the presence of complementary opposites in nature. This is a complex topic, rooted in what is most popularly known as the "wave-particle duality" in physics. Physicist Neils Bohr coined the term *complementarity* to describe this duality and he lectured widely on the topic toward the end of his life, showing how it applies to many areas of human concern beyond physics.[11]

This totality of all potentials is also called "the Worldfield," or just "the field." Out of the field, things come to be by means of concretion of opposites. For example, positive and negative energy come into being at the same time by virtue of their opposite nature, as do positive and negative electric charge.[12] Some consider the physical world the real world because it is the world of concrete existence. Yet the opposite view, that the field is the most real world, is just as true. In this view, the existing outer world, the world of contrasts, is only a part of a much fuller something (the field), *from which it comes into being when contrasts are brought forth.* We might say that the contrast world is the world that satisfies the intellect, which can only understand by perceiving contrasts, and the field is the world of the reality of the heart, though it is much greater than that, holding all possibilities for the future. Re-envisioning the cosmos with the heart means acknowledging the Worldfield, the Patterning, and its creative activity in our individual and collective lives.

What we usually call consciousness is more properly termed ego-consciousness. Our ego-consciousness and ego-knowledge in turn are more accurately called contrast-consciousness and contrast-knowledge, to distinguish them from the contents of the field.[13] To repeat, because the potentials of the cosmos are present in the field, and we have only uncovered a small bit of what it is possible to know, our highly prized contrast-knowledge, including our whole present scientific enterprise, is necessarily but a tiny bit of what will gradually come to a concrete, or contrast, knowing. We are able to develop knowledge by perceiving contrasts because opposites are present in the field; the field is in fact a *complexio oppositorum,* or complex of opposites

Consciousness, Freedom, and Love in a World of Becoming

At this point, we move closer to seeing that our ultimate heart-connection with the cosmos is the goal of the evolution of the cosmos.

> 6. *Something that is itself a potential of the cosmos brings opposites to concrete being. By analogy with our lives, we say we live unreflectingly when we are unaware of choices. Jung used the word* obstacles *for those events that force us to reflect.*[14]

This means that *obstacles engender consciousness.* The possibility of self-reflection by our human psyche presupposes an inherent structure in things (the Patterning), that is, something that can act as an obstacle to psychic energy and cause it to reflect, as a mirror is an obstacle in the path of light. Self-reflexivity is a latecomer in evolution, but it is central to consciousness and the self-understanding of the cosmos.[15] Our cosmos is evolutionary and is structured in such a way that there will be a flow from the field toward concrete conscious manifestation. It is a cosmos of becoming.

In *Answer to Job,* Jung demonstrates that moral obstacles or conflicts are what principally engenders consciousness.[16] As we become more conscious, we gain freedom. It is our contrast-knowledge that has given us our adaptability, the ability to transcend the limitations of the natural environment. Animals tend not to be able to survive a drastic change of environment, and so are "field-determined and unfree," as psychologist Erich Neumann puts it.[17]

The fact that the Big Bang is seen as the beginning of time makes it the symbolic representative of the divine obstacle which precipitated creation of the world of opposites, that is, which began the evolution of the whole. As obstacle, its meaning would be a supreme, if primordial, act of divine reflection. Every reflection is the creation of a *vis-à-vis.*[18] We will be looking at the possible meanings of God's *vis-à-vis* in chapters 4 and 5.

> 7. *The fundamental imbalance of the cosmos is the tilt towards consciousness. If the connection between the rise of consciousness and the moral dimension is valid, then perhaps we can find here a clue to the connection of consciousness and love. Gaining in consciousness increases freedom (as discussed above), and freedom is the gift of love. (See chapter 2 for more on this.)*

The mystic Jakob Boehme saw God as a Dark Fire that is the Nothing that wants to become Something.[19] If there is a tilt towards consciousness, then it would be reasonable to say either that the Creator intended that there be conscious creatures or that the Creator is unconscious and desires to become conscious. These two statements are not mutually exclusive.

Jung has demonstrated that the Self is both a God-image within humans and a "more comprehensive" potential personality that can draw the ego into its service.[20] Through the image of the Self and the universal experience of humanity that God has a personal aspect, we begin to sense a face in the cosmos. Jung's *Answer to Job* characterizes God as unconscious, or at least as failing to "consult the divine omniscience" as to Job's character. Instead, God plays "reprehensible" tricks on Job, at Satan's instigation.[21] Jung concludes that God displayed toward Job all the characteristics of a complete moral unconsciousness.

Jung also traces God's desire for "incarnation" to the fact that Job did not abjectly confess his guilt, but rather held fast to the integrity of his consciousness of his innocence. This, in Jung's view, became the obstacle that caused God to reflect upon the fact that Job held a morality that was superior to that which had permitted the "tests." In the Book of Job and in the "wisdom literature" that immediately followed Job in Hebrew writings, Jung saw the promise of the incarnation, as a response to Job's moral "challenge" to the Divine. It is as if Job's integrity has enabled God to remember wisdom and to continue on the path of becoming fully human. It was the cause of a further step in the evolution of consciousness, in the fulfillment of the evolutionary cosmos.

I know that all readers will not accede easily to these propositions. I can only recommend the works mentioned for deep study and meditation, as well as my own fuller analysis of Jung's *Answer to Job* in my book *The Web of the Universe*.[22] I believe, with Jung, that *qualities such as love and justice are a human assimilation of divine qualities in the field,* which are not truly actualized until they become human concerns.

Theologian Paul Tillich has been the prophet of "acceptance" in our time, both in his powerful sermon "You are Accepted" and in his book *The Courage to Be.*[23] His most comprehensive and concise statement from the latter is, "The courage to be is the courage to accept oneself as accepted in spite of unacceptability."[24]

We tend either to repress our consciousness of unacceptability or to wallow in it, either one of which blocks the evolution of consciousness. We feel either that there is no impediment to acceptability or that it is impossible. The difficult task, requiring courage, is to hold the opposites together, as Tillich puts it, to be accepted in spite of unacceptability. This means that both the acceptance and the unacceptability are real. Then our freedom is also real, being neither a freedom of the despair of the possibility of acceptance nor the happy-go-lucky assumption that acceptance is automatic. It is most significant that Tillich calls this "the courage to be," for his phrase emphasizes that true freedom is a matter of living with courage in the face of all that would daunt us, without repressing our consciousness of evil in the world and in ourselves. Our present project may help us to understand what God is after in all this.

I believe that as long as we have a potential for increased consciousness that arises out of what has happened to us and what we have done in our lives, we are sustained by the field. We are accepted. If we forfeit that potential, it is we who have cut ourselves off. We do indeed hurt others, and that is part of our unacceptability, but we can still grow.

It would seem that what God wants is not the freedom of pure unconsciousness or the freedom to repress our consciousness of evil, but rather the freedom of courage that a true moral consciousness enables in us. This is a form of the taking away of sin, or the bearing of sin, but God is the bearer of sin in us, as we become the bearers of God. To me there is no deeper manifestation of mutual love in the divine *vis-à-vis*.

> 8. *The internalization of God requires that we have an inner nature that is the umbilical from the field, through the Self, to our potential consciousness, which is born out of the Self. The continuity of evolution then requires our inner nature to be developed as a potential of spirit-matter that has been present from the beginning.*

This important aspect of our evolving spirit-matter cosmos is a consequence of the Anthropic Principle, which states that the physics in a cosmos with conscious, spiritually oriented beings must be such as to both permit and account for these phenomena. Teilhard de Chardin used the phrase "the within of things" to express his conviction that "inwardness" is one of the primal potentials of the cosmos.[25]

With regard to the field, the question of what is within and what is without must remain open. Neumann stresses that the very distinction of within/without is a product of contrast-knowledge, and therefore only a partial representation of reality.[26]

Item 3 of this chapter, that consciousness requires an organic being, and was therefore not present at the origin of our cosmos, lies behind the Anthropic Principle, as well as behind all of the rest of the eight points. The continuity of the evolution of life and the fact that consciousness is new, not ancient as we almost universally have imagined it, yields a fascinating and unprecedented picture.

CHAPTER 2

Self-Creating

I have felt the swaying of the elephant's shoulders;
and now you want me to climb on a jackass?
Try to be serious.

—MIRABAI, "Why Mira Can't Go Back to Her Old House"

We now need to look at the universe differently if we are to see it more fully. Re-envisioning the cosmos with the heart is not just an exercise in wish making; we simply have not seen it as well as we might, for we have looked primarily with the mind. The cosmos creates both naturally and abundantly in order that it may fulfill its being. We will learn to see it as self-creating in the advent and evolution of life, consciousness, and spirituality. That is, the coming to be of these things in the form of beings such as ourselves is part of the self-creation of the cosmos, so that it may finally *be* a cosmos, a unitary world. We live in a cosmos which is itself creative and which ultimately requires creativity of us.

Creativity is possible only where there is freedom. In this chapter, we will see that the foundation of freedom lies in the very nature of the "stuff of the universe." (This chapter is one of the three that focus the most on the known physical facts concerning the cosmos. The others are chapter 6, "Fostering," and chapter 7, "Physical Gathering and Layering.") A few sections will deal with the emerging transformation of physics, which is changing in such a way that it can recognize life and freedom in the universe as natural to that evolving stuff. Then we can apply our findings to human creativity and the emergence of value. Yet it should be no surprise that freedom and creativity are linked. A creative cosmos can only be self-consistent if it is free because a creative cosmos can never fail to generate something newer and deeper than anything that has ever been before. Its infinite depth could not show itself in any other way.

The fact that life has arisen—life that can be intelligent, civilized, and even loving when creatures are at their best—is creative enough in itself for a cosmos. But the life that has arisen manifests a much fuller creativity. Two qualities, unpredictability and newness, define creativity. Usually, though, we limit our use of the term to outcomes that we feel as positive. Of course, if something is new, it is also unique, alone. Nothing like it has existed before. Creativity is thus the hallmark of an individual thing, whether the creative something has come about through the efforts of a single being or of many working together. It is specific, unique, even if it is a new species.

I stress individuality here because the greatest transformations within humanity have arisen through creative individuals such as Buddha, Confucius, and Jesus, as well as other innovators. Of course, the transformation itself would not have followed had not greater numbers of people been ready for the innovations and had not conditions been favorable. The individuals concerned were creative sparks, igniting fires that fed on waiting fuel in the surrounding society. What is individual is what is different from its surroundings, and it requires the release of creativity and uniqueness to be different.

The fact that the record of evolution demonstrates the

emergence of new and unpredictable phenomena *prior to the advent of consciousness* is the basis for calling the whole cosmos creative. The emergence of consciousness itself then added a whole new dimension to the freedom displayed by the evolving "stuff of the universe" from the start. So we have two general levels of freedom, with the transition between them coming with the advent of what we now call consciousness.

In exploring the meaning of the fact that consciousness has arisen, I will conclude that the emergence and continuing growth of consciousness seem to epitomize the purposiveness of the cosmos.

Indeed, a new level of creativity is coming to actuality. It seems that the continued development of consciousness requires our participation. We have come to a place from which we inevitably participate, for good or ill, in the shaping of what we will become. Therefore, the universe ultimately demands creativity of us, along with whatever other sentient species are "out there," to fulfill its own being.

The Ground of Creativity

The fact that life has arisen implies that certain qualities are inherent in the nature of the physical reality within which we live. For newness to come about, not only in the form of life itself but in all its varieties, it must first be possible; there must be freedom. Our task is to come to an understanding of the cosmos that includes freedom as inherent to it so that life can exist. *The science of physics, as our understanding of matter, must not exclude life theoretically as a natural phenomenon.* Otherwise, it would be inadequate *as physics*. While this may seem obvious, the fact is that, until the advent of quantum mechanics in the 1920s, physical theory did indeed exclude life, being deterministic in attitude. With the growth of the quantum-mechanical view of atoms and their nuclei, the deterministic view is gradually being let go. Experimental investigation has uniformly favored quantum mechanics, and confirmation has only grown stronger with time.

Quantum mechanics did not, however, come about because of the need to include the possibility of life. That was simply a bonus. It came about as part of the effort to understand physical reality. It was an endeavor of the mind, grounded in the experimental results that it was invented to explain. The heart, or the feeling for the needs of life, was not an explicit part of the effort.

For a long while now, there has been another avenue of thinking, with deeper roots, that pushes toward the same conclusion: life is a fact for which we must account by making certain that physical theory includes the physical basis for life as a possibility. This requirement has recently come into its own as a study within physics under the name of the Anthropic Principle.

We have known that there must be a theory of matter that would enable us to describe matter-stuff as the carrier of life, but until fundamental experiments forced us to adopt the quantum-mechanical view, we could not have guessed how to find such a theory. It required modes of thinking that were too radically different from those of the past. We must now explicitly include the unsatisfied longings of the heart in visualizing physical reality. We must look at our physical roots to see where the evolution of our total being might take us. This means taking account of our highest aspirations, and discovering in the process at least some of the insights of the heart into the overall nature of things. If we find that we are being led to a heart-vision from a mind-vision, it means again that the heart-vision is, and always was, fundamental: the cosmos is a heart-cosmos, a cosmos of love.

Nonrationality

One of the crucial aspects of matter, discovered by physics in this century, is its nonrational nature. It is precisely this that "permits" life to develop. The quality of nonrationality arises in physics because, in order to give a complete description of some microphysical entity such as an electron or a photon, we are required to employ *logically contradictory* concepts. Logical contrasts are like ground and figure—that is, like the background of an engraving and its raised image. Usually, one concept forms the context for the contrasting form of its opposite, and the two do not mix, or at least in logic. For instance, good and evil are seen as opposites in the same manner: when good is the figure, evil is present as that from which good stands out. Similarly, when we focus on evil as figure, we automatically contrast it with the good as ground. At least, the logic of our minds functions in this way. The newly discovered (quantum) nature of physical reality means that, for the "objects" of microphysics, the figure always remains somewhat blended with the ground. We cannot obtain a fully rational contrast.[1]

An example of the nonrationality is that a particle such as a photon possesses the ability to take two different and discrete paths at once in going from point A to point B.[2] We cannot rationally speak of a single particle if it can take two or more different paths at once.

As mentioned in chapter 1, the model of the two logically contradictory properties is known as "wave/particle duality." A wave is not restricted from going by two paths at once, so we say that a photon "travels as a wave." But even though it travels as a wave, it shows up in experiments as a single point, or particle, which is precisely localized. Thus, we say that photons "interact as particles." In brief, a wave is something continuous, while a particle is discontinuous, so that the critical physical issue concerns the internal and external continuity of objects at the microphysical level. Continuity and discontinuity clearly are logically contradictory concepts, and both apply to the same entity.

The freedom of these and other fundamental building blocks

of nature to assume opposite, even logically contradictory, characteristics is now evident within physics. This freedom is another way to look at the ability of microphysical things to travel by more than one path from A to B at the same time. It is not rational. It is as if we each could leave a house by the front and back doors at the same time.

Something that is rational is determined: it is not free to be otherwise, due to the constraints of logic. Something undetermined is correspondingly nonrational. It is the same thing to say that something nonrational is free, at least free of logical constraints. I will continue to emphasize this contrast of freedom and determinism along the way.

The intellect, in its rational mode, favors determinism. To speak for the Anthropic Principle, even today, requires courage or heart. It is the same with the nonrational, an epithet with which the heart has been stigmatized, though it can indeed make excellent judgments. The difficulty of removing the stigma from the heart is compounded by the fact that other people stigmatize the intellect, so that a battle of sorts arises between the two camps. Both the ability of the heart to judge and of the intellect to see need to be granted and a treaty struck on this basis. The treaty would have the effect of blending or blurring the sharp figure-ground image we have had of intellect and emotion.[3] However, it is in full accord not only with the findings of modern physics but also with what we most deeply know of living. In the process of shifting our preconceptions, we are re-envisioning the cosmos with the heart. Though the heart can indeed be bound, in its essence it wants freedom.

Freedom

One of the earliest statements of the Anthropic Principle, from around 1930, was given by Teilhard de Chardin. He first says that many have tried to formulate a rational view of matter by considering it to be formed from deterministic elementary particles. He then says:

> *But this road leads nowhere.... Anyone who accepts this starting point blocks all roads that would bring one to the present state of the universe. On the other hand, from a cosmos formed and made up of elementary "freedoms" [atoms as described by quantum mechanics] it is easy to deduce ... all the appearances of exactitude upon which the mathematical physics of matter is founded.... The stuff of the universe is spirit-matter. No other substance than this could produce the human molecule.*[4]

Teilhard thus demands that we be able conceptually to begin with matter, atoms as known by physics, and find our way on this basis from the beginning of things to the "present state of the universe," namely, that it contains intelligent, aspiring, loving life.

Following his suggestion, I have worked to trace various qualities of human life as being "complexified" forms of qualities present in atoms.[5] Among these qualities is freedom. At the atomic level, one kind of evidence of freedom consists in the variety of states in which an atom can be. The word *state* is used in the ordinary sense of "condition," but that condition consists in having (containing) a certain amount of energy. It may seem remarkable that an atom can contain energy, but it does, in certain definite amounts.[6] The freedom is limited because it is a patterned freedom. The fact that the amounts of energy contained by the atom are definite gives rise to the idea of the *quantum*, which is Latin for a definite amount of something. (The plural is *quanta*.) Each definite amount of energy contained by the atom gives it a definite configuration or shape. Actually, it is more accurate to say that the energy amounts are definite because the patterns or configurations are definite. It is the electrons *in atoms* that assume the various shapes.

Another kind of freedom possessed by atoms is seen in the variety of paths by which they can change states. An atom has the "openness" and freedom to receive and emit energy quanta and to change its configuration in the process. Even the simplest of all elements, hydrogen, has hundreds of possible states, depending on how much energy it contains. In going from state to state, the path is not determined, though there are strong probabilities as to which path it will take. In the fact that certain paths are merely probable and not absolute, we feel a "loosening" of determinism, which might satisfy Teilhard's image of elementary freedom.

Most of all, however, freedom resides in the dual wave/particle character of the microphysical entities described above, and in the "Uncertainty Principle," which follows from the "complementarity" of the wave and particle natures. As mentioned in chapter 1, complementarity is the term applied by physicist Neils Bohr to describe the relationship of logically contradictory qualities that actually complement each other. That is, both qualities are needed for a description to be complete, even though they conceptually contradict each other. The Uncertainty Principle gives the measure of the limits imposed by the wave/particle duality on our knowledge of what the atoms are "doing." By alerting us to the limits on our ability to control or even to understand atoms, both the wave/particle duality and the Uncertainty Principle play major roles in our understanding of the living cosmos.

Spirit-Matter

One of the ideas in the above quotation from Teilhard de Chardin is that of spirit-matter. In order to give more of a sense of what this term means, I have included a representation of one of the hydrogen-atom states mentioned above (see figure 2.1).[7] We can

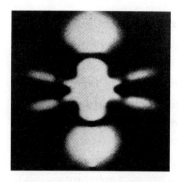

FIGURE 2.1 Model of electron pattern in hydrogen atom

see an elegant form, which is the *wave* shape of the single electron that fills most of the space of the atom. It has regions in which it is more dense than in other regions. *All of the electrons in atoms are in their wave state,* or as it is sometimes called, the quantum state.[8]

A wave, as noted earlier, is continuous with its surroundings. The wave form is "fuzzy" and indeed extends indefinitely. In *The Human Phenomenon,* Teilhard noted that, from this perspective, *every particle in the universe is coextensive with the universe.*[9] Here, in this overlapping of everything, is a concrete image of spirit that pervades all things and connects all beings. All of my electrons overlap all of yours at every moment of time. In the discussion of chemical bonds, just below, the concreteness of the wave will be seen. The wave *is* the electron.

The viewpoint of classical physics was that the electron was a hard-little-ball sort of particle. When quantum theory arrived, this archaic view was carried over somewhat into a picture of the same kind of ball traveling around the nucleus. In this view, the wave aspect of the electron shown in the picture represented a cloudlike clustering of probabilities as to where the electron (still conceived as a hard little ball) would most likely be found. This view of the "probability cloud," remnants of which still remain in physicists' use of language, has been shown to be bad physics. The wave is not an insubstantial something that "guides" the ball or gives the probability of its location. There simply is no ball in the cloud.[10]

An example of the application of the newer image of the electron is to be found in our better understanding of the nature of a given chemical bond. When we analyze a chemical bond we ask, "Is this bond best described in terms of the particle or wave aspect of the electron?"

We can explain some bonds as the attraction between positive and negative electric charges, but in the majority of cases this view is quite inadequate. Most bonds, especially those associated with life-molecules (DNA and proteins) involve the "sharing" of electrons between two atoms, with the electron itself as the bonding agent or glue. What sort of thing can be shared? If an electron were a particle in the sense of a hard, round, little ball, we would have to say that it spends some time near each atom in turn (see figure 2.2a).

Meanwhile, its attraction to either atom is always a direct straight line between the electron, wherever it is, with each of the nuclei of the two atoms being bonded. Under these circumstances, the picture becomes exceedingly complex, but in no case can we account for a bond with any strength against bending, which the bond is known to have. It is quite rigid and directional, as evidenced by the rigidity of crystals. The particle model of the bond fails completely.

Let me repeat this important fact: a bond is often rigid and directional. As water molecules freeze (bond) together, they must

FIGURE 2.2a Particle model of atomic bonds

FIGURE 2.2b Wave model of atomic bonds

attempt to assume specific orientations in direction with respect to other molecules. That they do this with great force is what enables water to break up rocks by freezing in cracks. As the freezing bonds form, they simply push in specific directions with their strength of expansion, breaking the rock.

If we visualize the bond in terms of the wave nature of the electron, we can picture the wave form enveloping and linking two atoms (see figure 2.2b). And because the bonding electron takes up its configuration with some force, it can have the required strength. Refer again to the definite shape assumed by the electron pattern shown in the photograph above.

In summary, the concepts of wave and particle are logically contradictory, but both belong to the same entity, the electron. Taken together, the two aspects make up a complete description. Therefore, physical theory now includes the nonrational, and this nonrationality introduces the freedom that is necessary in a physics that can support life.

The electron is a beautiful embodiment of the term *spirit-matter*, coined by Teilhard even before the pictures of hydrogen-atom states had been published. One can use the images in figures 2.1 and 2.2b for meditation on the unity of spirit and matter. The more one looks at them, the clearer it becomes that in the "stuff" that is represented by such images the spirit and matter aspects are inseparably blended.

Life and Newness

The human heart yearns for a fuller living beyond mere biological life. Indeed those creative individuals who have formed our notions of spirituality have tried to show us that a greater aliveness is possible, that not only they, but we too, can live more deeply. Our evolving, creative cosmos already includes much that is new—much more than simple growth, reproduction, and duration of existence. It also includes growth in intelligence and values and seems to be headed toward ever fuller consciousness and spirituality as well.

Indeed, once we admit the continuity of evolution, i.e., that living beings have evolved from the primordial stuff of the cosmos, we must find in spirit-matter and in the physics that is based on spirit-matter a foundation for the highest imaginable aspirations of finite beings, a life well beyond biological functioning, even infinitely beyond. Once the door to life is open, we must not only enter but envision the succeeding horizons of consciousness and spirituality, even the ultimate horizon, a process that I will describe in the chapter after next under the name "Godding."

Newness comes from within, from the fact that everything that grows and evolves eventually develops opposites. Historian of science Thomas Kuhn articulated this fact for scientific revolutions:

Normal science does not aim at novelties of fact or theory, and when successful finds none. New and unsuspected phenomena are, however, repeatedly uncovered by scientific research, and radical new theories have, again and again, been invented by scientists. History even suggests that the scientific enterprise has developed a uniquely powerful technique for producing surprises of this sort.[11]

Every time a scientific theory becomes "standard science," something develops from within to overturn it. The best known case is the transformation from Newton's physics to Einstein's. It is not widely known, however, in what way Einstein injected his most creative and transformative idea into physics. That idea was his introduction of symmetry considerations into physical theory as such. Einstein's new approach was so powerful that now, as the twentieth-first century begins, fundamental physics simply could not function without symmetry principles. At first, however, this creative move brought derision: Einstein was accused of abandoning physics for art. Symmetry is one of those novelties that exemplify the "radical new theories" Thomas Kuhn mentioned, against which standard science fiercely defends itself.

Kuhn's conclusion strongly suggests an aspect of the creative cosmos: the more we work with and probe into what we think we understand, the more we uncover hidden contradictions. The most radical case to date is the discovery of the ultimately contradictory nature of microphysical objects as described above. Our attempt to understand reality moves us forward from contradiction to new contradiction, for contradictions are both inherent in reality itself and likely to arise in the contrast between new knowledge and past, how we have understood things.

We might say that the cosmos has an endless capacity to defy our projections as to what it really is. The more we run into these contradictions, the more creativity is demanded of us in the attempt to understand them. We move from newness to newness as we grow in depth, and in so doing, we encounter more and more freedom through situations that force us to choose between nondeterministic opposites. It certainly enhances freedom to be able to use more and different concepts in the theory of physical reality, and if we find we need to use logical opposites, we are free to conceptualize in one way or its opposite.

For example, quantum mechanics was developed in two forms, one based on the wave picture and one on the particle view. Only later were they shown to be mathematically equivalent, so that we may now use either, whichever is more convenient in the case at hand. That is a form of freedom. No other view could do justice to the contradictions that abound in all areas of life. One instance is medical ethics, where our ability to prolong life becomes an ethical justification for prolonging a meaningless vegetative existence in the dying. Similar contradictions can be found in every other area of life as well.

Creativity and Individuality

Humans have much in common, not only in outward form but in inward form: we have highly similar psychological structures. We say we are individuals, but while we can see our individuality physically, what we have in common often dominates. The very existence of a science of psychology depends on a large portion of our behavior being collective, the same or very similar for all. Paradoxically, however, as human beings, one thing we possess in common is a capacity for creativity, for self-expression that is different, unique, at whatever level of activity we live. This is a direct consequence of the eternal presence of opposites in all things, such as we have been describing in the case of atoms.

Creativity is individual behavior producing variation, doing the unexpected, the unclassifiable. We picture tribal life as continuing in stable forms over thousands of years. Within that unchanging framework, there was provision for misdemeanor, penance, and punishment. But as long as no new idea arose that attracted a substantial group to new behavior in defiance of accepted codes, there was no serious disturbance. Yet from time to time, such newness did develop, probably through the same sort of process that brings about scientific revolutions, though it developed much more slowly. The three creative individuals mentioned earlier, Buddha, Confucius, and Jesus, brought new discoveries in the same sense. Our cosmos is one that develops novelty in the midst of stability.

To describe millennia of change in a few words, innovation leads to diversity, in which opposing behaviors can be seen side by side. Until such is the case, the stable codes carry the principal authority. But when two new potential authorities collide, when a whole new way of living is visible in contrast to the conventional milieu, then the individual must decide between the two. In that act the individual carries the authority alone and also has the freedom to choose. In such a decision, the individual re-envisions the cosmos with the heart. In tribal life, this is a totally new and disturbing happening. We can thus see how consciousness arises through collisions of duty, or of authorities, as experienced by individuals. I have been deliberately describing "tribal" life, but as Einstein noted, we still are living that way for the most part. He observed:

Few people are capable of expressing with equanimity opinions which differ from the prejudices of their social environment. Most people are even incapable of forming such opinions.[12]

In other words, we tend to sacrifice or avoid the choices that would be ours if we only saw the diversity of contradictory values around us, especially now that the world is small and we have access to information as to how things are done in various cultures.

It is easier to do things as everyone else nearby does them. This is what is meant by "living unconsciously." On a given day, we wake up and do our work, pay attention to traffic, etc.; but we do it somewhat mechanically, and to that extent we must be classified as unconscious (as always, I include myself). Of course, at our level of development, we need some routine or our living would be chaotic. The question is whether and where our routine ways of doing things cause us to miss something that might be of great value to us personally, if we were to exercise the courage to make some radical change in our way of living that would break away from the collective worldview all around us. In our unconsciousness, we might even be forfeiting the discovery of a value system that could transform a local, regional, or global outlook, for there have indeed been such innovations throughout history.

What we need to do is get variety into our lives. Psychologist and poet Sheila Moon said, "The hallmark of consciousness is creativity." Of course, just *any* change is not necessarily creative. Change that is creative involves a positive re-envisioning of values. The question regarding truly individual behavior is what is the new step that increases the value and meaning of life, especially taking into account the fact that one is not alone. That is, though it is possible to live our own lives creatively while the rest of the community just goes on in its rut, sometimes we come upon values that might possibly benefit many more people than just us. That is the origin of our urge to share our ideas with others.

In fact, it should be a criterion of our value system that we feel that the values we hold would improve things if others adopted them, so that we are not just trying to exploit the unconsciousness of those around us to do as we please. Imagine, for instance, that I believe I should be able to weave in and out of lanes as I drive and that I think that other drivers are dunces for driving so stolidly. In that case, my values would not transfer to a wider group. The general situation would not be improved if the majority drove as I did. (This is a mundane example, but significant to me nonetheless, for I have indeed felt the way I have just described.)

I value religious pluralism, in part because I feel that, if a significant portion of the rest of all people valued it, there would be a significant reduction in religious strife. Naturally, values are much more than simple intellectual statements. They must be heart-things if they are to be effective. In order to make it clearer why religious pluralism is transferable, I will compare it to a value that is not: I often have the passing feeling that things would be greatly improved if others voluntarily adopted my complete religious outlook. But that feeling differs greatly from my belief in the value of religious pluralism because a religious outlook is a very personal thing. Religious pluralism preserves the intimately personal nature of the religious outlook, while addressing the interpersonal aspect of living.

Our individual viewpoints must expand more and more to include the rest of the cosmos, in what might be called a pluralistic heart: family and friends, yes, but also the rest of humanity. If one is an initiator of new value, of a value that takes hold for a considerable time, it is because others see the value and desire to carry it on, to integrate it into their living. One might object that from this point of view the religious demagogues Jim Jones and David Koresh were just such innovators, that "new values" can be destructive. But their value experiments faded out, as I believe destructive values eventually do. The seventy-year dominance of Communism in Europe lasted a considerable time from the point of view of the many humans who lived and died entirely within that span. But as things turned out, Communism simply was not sustainable. Our values should be sustainable, just as our use of natural resources should be. No values can be permanent, but they should be conceived as durable.

Values

British journalist and author J. Middleton Murry, in his book *God*, put the description of value in what I feel are some of the clearest possible terms:

> *"Value" is creative newness in the organic process of the universe; more than this, it is creative newness which maintains itself. And this self-maintenance of creative newness must necessarily be measured, not by the life of the individual [who brings it], but by the life of the whole. . . . "Values" are always organic in origin. A poem or a temple which maintains itself as an object of response was once the organic extension of its creator.*[13]

A value—that is, *what one values*—is *a form into which psychic energy flows*, whether in art, ethics, or religion. It engages one's feelings as something "right."

One who creates something valued by others still does so from a deep, personal place. The artist Kandinsky called it "inner necessity," which is a fine expression of what Murry calls the "organic" origin of value. We speak commonly of what "she has it in her" or "he has it in him" to do, reflecting the same recognition expressed by Murry. A work of art remains part of the organic totality of the originator, in the sense that we recognize the work of a composer or painter. Together they, the creator and the work of art, form a "metabiological" unity, reflecting the metabiological unity of the biological person. Murry used the term "metabiological unity" regarding a person in much the same way in which we now speak of psychological wholeness.[14]

What lasts as art is what comes from the place of wholeness in the artist, whether or not the artist as person has achieved a comprehensive integration. As is best seen in the experience of such artists as Marc Chagall, Isamu Noguchi, or Georgia O'Keeffe, the very doing of the art effects the integration of the personality through the contact between the artist's ego and the center that Jung (as we have noted above) called "the Self," the archetype of completeness. The metabiological unity comes about in this manner.

In humans, the Self is our deepest psychic "regulator," which brings about our fateful encounter with those opposites that we have neglected in our lives, especially in the formation of habits that leave us "one-sided."

The fact of our biological unity or coherence is obvious. What is not obvious to most of us is the equally valid fact that we are each personally beset with psychological disunity; our lives are not psychologically whole. Murry also notes that our lives cannot have a full psychological wholeness unless they are also as far as possible consonant with the nature of the universe. One can and must, however, start where one is, for we do not know fully the nature of the universe but can only trust that, as we gain understanding, that understanding gets closer to reality.

To return to the work of art, it too must be consonant with the life of the whole group, culture, or world, or it will not maintain itself. If it not only expresses the central value of the artist but also carries interpersonal value, it wins widespread response. Murry, continuing the remarks quoted above, articulates what it means to re-envision the cosmos with the heart:

> *Value is the variation of proven maximum significance in the organic evolution of the whole during the period which most nearly concerns us. Our duty is simply to help it to come; and our method of doing our duty is to maintain the variation in ourselves, by achieving our own metabiological unity. Only thus can we secure ourselves against the danger of becoming reversional in the organic process of the whole.*
>
> *Values are simply those organic creations in the life-process to which there is response. Values, we repeat once more, are variations which maintain themselves. There are no other values.*
>
> *The significance of a person's own metabiological life depends on the significance of the variations which that person embodies and transmits. That will be judged not in the person's lifetime, or by others. Life itself will ultimately pronounce upon us: We became a significant variation, or we reverted.*
>
> *We can incorporate the universe to ourselves, or ourselves to the universe; which is the same thing. The biological organism becomes an organism on a higher level. Through this metabiological organism Life can create, without hindrance, her own pure and inscrutable newness.*
>
> *It is, in short, our privilege and burden that we alone among organisms must learn, slowly and painfully, to be an organism.*[15]

As I see it, there is absolutely no doubt that for an individual to learn to be an organism—to be one single person rather than a mass of unreconciled desires and actualities—is a slow and painful process. We tend not even to see our own inner contradictions. In *Purity of Heart is to Will One Thing,* Kierkegaard gave as his prime criterion the question, "Are you conscious of living as an individual?"[16] That is, are your actions and motives your own, rather than automatically those of your friends, your community, your ethnic background, or your nation? An individual may well hold values that are similar to those of groups of which she or he is a member. In that case, the critical issue is the examination of values in depth by the person involved. As psychologist Elizabeth Boyden Howes has said, "You are centered when you can go either way."[17]

A Nonrational Consistency

The several areas of living that we have been discussing are all consistent in this one point: the opposites with which they deal are nonrational. This consistency holds in the cosmos as a whole, in the world of microphysics, and in the diverse claims of authority upon us in everyday life. The heart-point is that we are indeed free, but we must sacrifice an ultimate rationalism even to see it. The nonrationality of all of the opposites that we face could be argued at length, if space were available, but I hope that simply thinking about it in the following terms will help make it clear. If a rational choice were possible, rather than a heart-choice from within a milieu of conflicting values, then there would be a unique, *correct* solution to the question as to what is the right view of the universe and all the details of our life within it. If the answer to things were to be found in the realm of the rational, then only one religious authority would ultimately dominate, or rather it would be the final quenching of all religion. Sooner or later, some super-smart person would figure out the whole scheme of things and tell us, and that would be the end of thinking!

The cosmos seems, rather, to be such that the involvement of each of us is required. That involvement is, in part, our response to values that will determine which new approaches to living will be maintained, or in Murry's terms, which will indeed be values. There is nothing to guarantee that the choice that I consider to be best ultimately will be found to be right. That is just what it means to be free. A value will only be sustained or not sustained in and by people. Seen in this light, it feels like a profound trust on God's part. But is that not exactly the nature of God's love: that we are free? A world of conflict is the only kind of world in which free acts of love are possible. Thus, to create such a world is the supreme act of love. But can our heart-vision even receive this, when the created world is so full of pain?

Whether we say that the possibility of love is engendered by the basic freedom inherent in spirit-matter or that a physical cosmos that inherently possesses in spirit-matter is engendered by a God who is love—it makes no difference. In either case, nonrational freedom provides the point of consistency of the cosmos. How each of us experiences consistency is extremely important, for that embodies our individual wholeness. In this book, I am writing my own view of a consistent universe, which will be different from that of someone else. It moves me, so I want to share it.

One of the things that my vision suggests to me is that, in a cosmos that continually produces opposites "from within," the arising of consciousness out of the primordial unconscious material, or of life from what is apparently unliving, is only natural, for the inexhaustibility of contradiction, i.e., the ultimate nonrationality of things, speaks to me of the inexhaustibility of complexity and of consciousness.

Contradictions lie in wait throughout nature, so as nature evolves, more and more creative responses are demanded. The most successful adaptation will be achieved by those with the most comprehensive worldview, but once again continuity of evolution indicates that this process started with the simplest kind of adaptive behavior, such as the stimulus-response activity of one-celled creatures.

Indeed, this selectivity of adaptation is another point of consistency in the operation of nature at all evolutionary levels, and I believe that it therefore must continue in effect. New values have a way of leading us out of our previous selves and onward in the general transformation of life. For those who prefer any one of the world's religions, that religion had a beginning and was sustained because it proved transformative for many people. Any religion must continue to serve that function or die out. Our cosmos is self-transcendent, in the very fact that it is fundamentally in disequilibrium, as was pointed out in chapter 1.

A consistent universe will not suddenly change character, say, from nonrational to rational. We may have "quantum leaps" in our understanding of the cosmos, of course, but the nature of progress is that we deepen our understanding of what we already know. The facts remain the same, regardless of how we interpret them, and it is the same universe before and after we see it newly. In our lives also, consistency is much deeper than rationality, and we remain ourselves in spite of our frequent attempts to deceive ourselves as to who we are. In our intuition we know this, and we also know that we are part of a cosmos that holds its course.

We know that the cosmos is nonrational, and consistently so, with virtually the same degree of knowing as the degree to which we know that Earth is round and not flat. I mention this because I have heard of theologians who seem to expect a sudden change in the natural order sometime. That seems to me equivalent to accusing God of bad design. On the other hand, a cosmos that is capable of continual newness or creativity corresponds to a theological view in which God never runs out of new moves. If it is now a universe of newness and if it is not to change character, then it will always be creative. There will be no final ringing down of a curtain saying that the play is over.

I believe that this viewpoint also demands of us much more responsibility for the outcomes of our choices—and even for the shaping of the next stages in the development of consciousness. We need to practice using our hearts, for the answers will not come from the head alone. Ever more profound choices will be set before us, and as has been recorded in innumerable passages from the world's scriptures, the choices will involve the enhancement or the crippling of life.

CHAPTER 3

Unfolding Beauty

*Split the Lark—and you'll find the music—
Bulb after Bulb, in Silver rolled—
Scantily dealt to the Summer Morning
Saved for your Ear when Lutes be old.*

*Loose the Flood— you shall find it patent—
Gush after Gush, reserved for you—
Scarlet Experiment! Sceptic Thomas!
Now, do you doubt that your Bird was true?*

—EMILY DICKINSON

We have just briefly explored creativity as a very real quality of our physical cosmos, though seeing it that way is an unusual approach to describing cosmic things. Here I want to work with another unusual idea—that the cosmos is in the process of leading, or drawing, consciousness out of its unconscious matrix, leading us out of our unconscious self-involvement.

It is the beauty of the universe that draws us out of our dark shells into the light. True, our planet is beautiful and draws us out of ourselves to meet it, but the night sky opens to us the sense of a larger depth and wonder, the vision of the cosmos as a whole.

Sometimes, seeing beauty is not easy. Much of modern art shows the terrifying or chaotic as beauty, and we need only to recall the testimony of Jacques Lusseyran, which I quoted earlier, as to the beauty he found in Buchenwald. In this chapter, we will face again this challenge of opening ourselves to new, and perhaps difficult, ways of seeing, for many of our true souls remain deeply hidden, and we require courage even to see that which might draw us out into fuller participation in life. Yet the cosmos is unfolding and doing so now in previously unimaginable ways. We simply cannot take repose in a vision that comprises only more of the same. I hope that this will become much clearer in this chapter.

A Call from Within

The earliest philosophies acknowledged curiosity as a human given, but curiosity and alertness go back well before human origins. Curiosity and alertness are heart-qualities, and the ability of the cosmos to draw us out is a heart-quality as well. Thus, all these qualities belong to the re-envisioning. The heart knows, in its deep places, that it is being led out from within, that there is a call. The call is from the depths, even though we may hear it as a call from elsewhere to go toward and explore the depths of the universe. In the end, those depths are right here, where we are.

Whatever or whoever is calling us out acts, as it were, on the assumption or trust that there is something inside us worthy of discovery and bringing forth, namely, the individual self as a strong, interested, and choiceful person. It wants *us*, as individuals, to explore *it*. Paradoxically, this is the inner movement of the need to be oneself, which is felt to be among the more difficult human achievements. Often our wounds prevent us from assuming or trusting it ourselves. Philosopher Martin Buber relates that Rabbi

Zusya once said: "In the coming world, they will not ask me: 'Why were you not Moses?' They will ask me: 'Why were you not Zusya?'"[1] Each of us knows that we somehow keep our true being hidden and that much of the possibility for fullness of living is sacrificed in that hiding.

In letting the beauty in the cosmos affect us, we are, so to speak, coming out to meet it. In the process, we make ourselves vulnerable. Sometimes things that are psychically powerful, either in attraction or repulsion, overwhelm us, but even then it is an opening of our souls—an unfolding of our being.

Whether we feel that we really become ourselves depends on whether we have the experience of participating in meaning, which is very close to the experience of beauty.[2] Though less poetic than Keats' version, the equation, "Beauty is Meaning; Meaning, Beauty," is more accurate, because both sides of the equation represent actual human experiences. I am assuming that we do not identify beauty with pleasantness but rather follow the lead of art: beauty is an aspect of that which philosopher Rudolf Otto called "the numinous," which can be terrifying as well. The concept of numinosity is a combination of the *mysterious* and the *tremendous*.[3]

Is the Cosmos Hostile?

Our view of the cosmos has strong effects on human culture. As we discovered in the course of the twentieth century that the universe is vastly greater in extent than anyone had imagined, we also have seen scientists and others concluding that humanity is negligible in the cosmos and that the universe is fundamentally meaningless. For example, Nobel laureate Steven Weinberg closes his book *The First Three Minutes* (describing the origin of our cosmos in the Big Bang) with the thought that ours is an "overwhelmingly hostile universe." In his opinion,

> *It is even harder to realize that this present universe has evolved from an unspeakably unfamiliar early condition, and faces a future extinction of endless cold or intolerable heat. The more the universe seems comprehensible, the more it also seems pointless.*
>
> *But if there is no solace in the fruits of our research, there is at least some consolation in the research itself. Men and women . . . build telescopes and satellites and accelerators, and sit at their desks for endless hours working out the meaning of the data they gather. The effort to understand the universe is one of the very few things that lifts human life a little above the level of farce, and gives it some of the grace of tragedy.*[4]

Needless to say, I do not share these views. Since we are here and have been nurtured on an Earth that has proved favorable to the development of life for over four billion years, how can we draw a conclusion that the universe is "overwhelmingly hostile?" Others, such as physicist Freeman Dyson, conclude that the cosmos is "unexpectedly hospitable."[5]

The point I am making is that our view of the cosmos does indeed have an impact on our view of life and the meaning of human culture. And the view we adopt says a lot about us as the viewer. To re-envision the cosmos with the heart or to find the heart in the cosmos (which is the same thing) then entails re-envisioning ourselves in a similar fashion.

Love Brings Forth

The universe brings forth freely and abundantly, in forms innumerable. We are struck by the beauty of nature as much in the power of storms and earthquakes as in the interplay of light, trees, stones, and water. It often takes a special effort to see the beauty of nature when its killing hand strikes near to our own homes, but we must interweave our fear of such power with awareness that it reflects the freedom and creativity of the cosmos. We must also see human darkness as part of this same dark side of "nature."

The question of how the cosmos drew us forth, along with all other forms of life, and drew forth something now approaching consciousness from our previous, more primitive, state can perhaps best be approached if we look first at how we are brought forth as persons by those who were here before us, our parents and teachers.

When newborn kittens are lovingly handled by humans for about twenty minutes a day, they open their eyes on the average twenty percent sooner and leave the nest to explore sooner in the same proportion. They are *led out* by the supportive attention which is given to them, ready to meet the world and eager to explore the unknown. Loving attention brings humans forth as well. Humans need soul handlers, so that they may be willing to perceive and engage the world, unencumbered by rationalistic or authoritarian protective emotional shells. To develop the needed attitude of open eyes and readiness to explore the unknown requires loving preparation. The qualities of openness and self-motivation amount to the same thing.

Openness and Self-Motivation

Openness is not merely acceptance of everything that comes along. Human living is not so simple as that, for if we were freely accepting of all, we would be open to self-deception and to deception by others. In that sense, *to love is to strengthen the beloved.* The oldest living things on Earth, the bristlecone pines, live under the harshest weather conditions at the tops of mountains, adding an inch of rings in a century. Is it then love that gives them their endurance and beauty? Our puzzle of seeing the cosmos as loving has now taken a new turn of complexity. Where one person may see the conditions under which the bristlecone pines grow as hostile, another might see them as a gift of great value. Perhaps our greatest need with regard to openness is to learn acceptance of the beauty hidden in harsh circumstances. When we falter in this, we might consider the beauty of a face well-weathered by a difficult life.

We might also ask how often we take the easy way and leave the difficulties to others, demanding nothing of ourselves. Key to the concept of openness is the manner in which, and the extent to which, we employ the critical principle, which is the principle of *doubt*. This may sound paradoxical, for at first view openness might seem to be the absence of doubt, which is absolute trust. But we doubt when we want really to be sure of what we know, which means being open to whatever possibility really is the case, so far as can be determined. To doubt is to desire a deeper look. Doubt asks what the possibilities are for alternative explanations.

A knowledge of something that can be known will always supersede a belief in that same thing and will be felt as more satisfying. It is the strength of holding one's own, making certain that one can hold things at arm's length and look at them, that enables one actually to be open to them without feeling, in a sense, violated by them. Doubting is not only an exercise of tremendous value; it is absolutely necessary for us if we are to move to deep heart-understanding, whether of ourselves or the cosmos. I like to think of the activity of doubting as loving the truth, which we do not *in spite* of truth's elusive nature, but precisely *because* truth is hard to gain.

The cosmos unfolds beauty to the extent that we indeed seek the truth of its depths, but it does not just hand us the key to its being. Rather, it tests our desire to know it more fully. Therefore, its beauty is as subtle as that of the weathered tree or the elder of a human community, which motivates us to seek truer wisdom. The love that moves us in this way comes from the cosmos wanting to be known.

Along with what we identify as a will to live, we have a will to *be alive*, which is closely related to being ourselves and shares the same difficulties of actualization. The will to live is merely a bodily or animal tenacity with respect to our continued existence. Most of us can satisfy that drive, but the issue of being personally alive engages us at a different level. It is indeed rare that we open ourselves fully to others and are truly present and alive. We are stuck inside ourselves and need to be led out. In order for this situation to be transformed, we must find or be shown something which evokes our interest, which grabs or grips us, so that, when we move toward something in our lives, we do so from our own inner motivation. If we look at numerous cases of self-motivated people, we will generally see that each is drawn toward something perceived as beautiful. That is awakening, or rather being awakened by a call.

Beauty is a general term for that which draws or leads us out of our shells. Beauty is as much a feature of the universe as is creativity. It is, of course, something within ourselves that we project onto our surroundings, including the vast array of stars in the night sky. But that kind of connectedness of things inner and outer is inherent in the whole nature of reality and is an aspect of the cosmos that leads us out. There is a beautiful myth of the Native Americans of the Northwest coast, in which the creator spirit, Raven, taps with his bill on the shell of an oyster, gently calling the creature out, not for food, but to be alive in the world, to be a friend and part of the family of life.

For many of us, nature is obviously beautiful, which is to say that it does indeed draw us forth. There is variation, elaboration, unfolding. We are always finding more there than we had known. It is essentially interesting and profound. Most of us find human effort, skill, and mastery beautiful, whether physical, as in sports; intellectual, as in literature; or both, as in musical performance. The experience of beauty is a feeling dimension underlying all of these. My own effort in this book is toward presenting what is beautiful to me, hoping that its reality will move others into a fuller living.

The Beauty of Thinking

It may seem that critical thought kills the mystery of things. Modern physics' great lesson to the contrary is the discovery, through the most thorough application of critical thought, of the essentially nonrational nature of physical reality, which was discussed in the previous chapter. In this case, critical thought has not lessened the mystery of the cosmos but rather increased it. Critical tools can play a major role in re-envisioning the cosmos with the heart, as long as they are indeed used to bring out *meaning*.

Here is an example of creative analysis of poetry that does this. It is one I used for many years in science classes for nonscientists, to show the possibility that meaning need not be destroyed by analysis. The experiment is as follows: first, just read (preferably aloud) William Blake's poem, "The Sick Rose":

> *O Rose, thou art sick!*
> *The invisible worm*
> *That flies in the night,*
> *In the howling storm,*
>
> *Has found out thy bed*
> *Of crimson joy:*
> *And his dark secret love*
> *Does thy life destroy.*[6]

Now read the following analysis, which represents the complete commentary on this poem by the editors of the anthology in which it appears:

> *The reader who takes the rose in this poem to be a conventional symbol for love or for beauty or for both, is still faced with the problem of what the worm symbolizes. Whatever it is, it is not good. By devoting as much of his poem to the worm as to the sick rose, Blake communicates images of nastiness that are quite different from the pretty images in Herrick's poem on the same subject. [Herrick's poem begins, "The rose was sick and, smiling, died," and goes on to describe the funeral rites performed by "the sweet and flowery sisterhood."] The adjective in-visible suggests that the worm comes from the unseen world of evil; real worms do not make "dark secret love." The "howling storm" suggests a catastrophe far greater than the destruction of a literal rose. Blake's worm seems to symbolize the unseen forces that destroy love and beauty: materialism, greed, hypocrisy, deceit, prudery, neurosis—the list is endless. The symbol cannot be paraphrased as one particular evil; Blake apparently used a symbol because it enabled him to suggest many kinds of evil.*[7]

Now give voice to the poem again and see whether it feels different and, if so, how. The commentary was helpful, was it not? Actually, it just begins to touch the depth of the poem, but it suggests directions of thinking, leading to fuller feeling, which we can pursue on our own or with others. The crucial thing is to begin and end with the poem and only use analysis as a means of appreciation, not an end in itself, which is where the heart gets lost. In re-envisioning the cosmos, the crucial thing is to begin and end with how the cosmos affects us as living human beings.

"But," one might ask, "doesn't analysis have to stop somewhere? Isn't it necessary to stop thinking sometime and just give your heart to something?" To this my response is that to doubt conscientiously is to give your heart to truth, or better, to beauty and meaning.

Only the principle of doubt, applied in many areas of our lives, will produce solid knowledge, of which we can now be assured will not exterminate the mystery of things. Only such solid knowledge will afford the security upon which to live with the openness needed to see through illusion, and not only illusion, but also the plateaus and short-circuits in our progress as human beings: money, power, sex, success, etc. But though it is greatly needed, knowledge is only a part of the leading out process, as noted earlier.

Would we not all feel more safe in a world in which the citizens were able to perceive realities and to reason about them? In which people took steps not be deceived as to the facts by anyone who happened to make a claim (such as a local politician, a president of the United States, or a head of state of another nation)? Would not such a world be far more beautiful? The aim is for the individual to clarify her or his own values and to develop the self-motivation to live according to them by finding meaning in doing so. We can only see which of our values are strong within ourselves by exposing them to the greatest variety of points of view.

Along the way, our inherent inner beauty begins to surface and to shine. Each of us has a uniqueness that defies classification and a true heart that is the source of our deepest feelings. It is unfortunately true that these feelings often are suppressed by external authorities in family, religious, and school settings, to say nothing of how they are suppressed by traumas and tragedies.

Dark Beauty

Beauty is not devoid of conflict, but that truth simply affirms what has been said above concerning the value of conflict in our being led out from within. What about a great jewel—a piece of nature that has been enhanced through human effort and mastery? Yes, it is beautiful, but now it is something that more often than not is pursued only for its monetary value, so the motive in desiring it may not be nearly as pure as the stone! It would be easy to avoid consciousness of the fact that the motives attached to a beautiful object can be in conflict.

Is a nuclear explosion beautiful? Awesome power can be beautiful; even death can be beautiful. But the combination of a nuclear explosion and death is horrible to contemplate. All forms of beauty can be misused and can be pursued even in horrified fascination. Here, again, we are touching upon the numinous. It is *numinosity* that grips us, with its sheer destructive power as well as its sublime holiness. These are inherent properties of our cosmos, or we would not have been led out into their contemplation.

It is a dangerous thing to free the individual, but *setting free is the precise meaning of love.* I know well how difficult it is to come to this feeling with respect to persons and things we love. We do not want to lose them; we cannot let go of our possessiveness. But how often it is just that sense of possession that costs us the thing in question. Love, beauty, freedom, life: all are dangerous, but worth the venture. If we die young in the process, how much better than to live to great age without having stirred the dragon to waking!

Many aspects of political and religious systems are designed to "contain" the individual, to make him or her feel comfortable and to restrain him or her. Shakespeare gives the following lines to Julius Caesar:

> *Let me have men about me that are fat;*
> *Sleek-headed men and such as sleep o' nights.*
> *Yond' Cassius has a lean and hungry look;*
> *He thinks too much: such men are dangerous.*[8]

We fear that freedom will become license, and so it may. On the other hand, lack of freedom kills meaning and beauty.

At the end of the twentieth century, we witnessed a resurgence of passion for democracy in nations in which it had been long suppressed. This demonstrates the great capacity for self-regulation of the collective psyche, by means of the power of the opposites. At the same time, however, we see the release of some of the most barbaric attitudes arising from ethnic and religious issues. Most of the hatreds couched in ethnic terms are probably religious issues at core.

In the individual, too, *all* of the opposites have potential, both the creative and the dark components; but unless the damage to the individual psyche has been too great, we can and must learn how to help people to handle them. For this, a sense of beauty is essential, including the beauty of risking for the sake of something great. Unfortunately, virtually none of our endeavor has been directed to such ends, and we still largely qualify for Jung's epithet "barbarian" in the following:

> *We are still so uneducated that we actually need laws from without, and a task-master of Father above, to show us what is good and the right thing to do. And because we are still such barbarians, any trust in the laws of human nature seems to us a dangerous and unethical naturalism. Why is this? Because under the barbarian's thin veneer of culture the wild beast lurks in readiness, amply justifying his fear. But the beast is not tamed by locking it up in a cage.* There is no morality without freedom. *When the barbarian lets loose the beast within him, that is not freedom but bondage. Barbarism must first be vanquished before freedom can be won. This happens, in principle, when the basic root and driving force of morality are felt by individuals as constituents of their own nature and not as external restrictions. How else are we to attain this realization but through the conflict of opposites?*[9]

Perhaps we do know that we need opposites for completeness, but we may not know that we need to permit their conflict within ourselves to grow and become civilized. Often, this means that we must permit ourselves to become conscious of how they do in fact conflict in our lives. We usually tend to avoid all awareness of the conflict of these opposites, but then we miss the civilizing effect of struggling with them. Some of the major opposites needed for human wholeness are: masculine and feminine, heart and mind (emotion and intellect), light and darkness (including knowing and unknowing), spirit and matter, self and other, introversion and extraversion, individual and community, past and future, time and eternality.

In the past, ability to simultaneously hold opposites has been the prerogative of God. The divine opposites included universal/personal, love/wrath, present/remote, masculine/feminine, accounting/forgiving, and same/other. But we, too, are beginning to permit some of these to come to conflict in our own lives. When we consciously give each pole of a pair equal weight, then we can no longer take the old easy choices.

If we decide the universe manifests something we want to call "God," then all of these opposites are essential aspects of the God-model. With respect to any of the pairs of opposites, it is interesting to imagine all the freedom we possess for both creativity and destruction as the gift of a loving God—so loving as not to will to violate our freedom even to save us from ourselves! After all, this great human experiment has survived so far in spite of its terrible struggles. In that sense, the cosmos is indeed hospitable. Dangers are more pressing today, but unless we *all* join the human race with our hearts, through our *openness to all that is indeed human*—all these warring opposites—humanity will remain unfulfilled as a concept, even if it does not self-destruct. The beauty of humanity in the fullness of these conflicts is indeed terrifying, like that of a storm.

And, of course, if humanity were fulfilled on Earth, then it would be prepared for the next terrifying step toward oneness with the universe.

There is an important link between freedom and consciousness, because a true consciousness is only attained through a transformation in which we accept responsibility for what we are and do. Jung put it most succinctly in a letter; his comment supplements the quotation just above:

> *Where you are not conscious, there can obviously be no freedom. Through the analysis of the unconscious, you increase the amount of freedom. A complete consciousness would mean an equally complete freedom and responsibility. If unconscious contents approaching the sphere of consciousness are not analysed and integrated, then the sphere of your freedom is even diminished through the fact that such contents are activated [anyway] and gain more compelling influence upon consciousness than when they were completely unconscious.*[10]

If we really were to attempt to educate our offspring toward unique personality, i.e., really attempt to lead them out from within themselves, then we would help them precisely in the area we have been dealing with, namely, awareness of inner conflict and response to those conflicts that would *bring forth their own inherent values*, trusting the person and the values in the process. Such an approach really would substitute for a great deal of the "analysis of unconscious contents" mentioned by Jung, for its purpose is precisely to bring what is "inside" into the realm of consciousness. Most concretely, this would occur in the form of challenges to unconscious cultural assumptions. Of course, as Jung implies, there is much more than merely cultural mindsets to be dealt with in many individuals. To gain more freedom, more must be brought to light from within. One important point is that the leading-out process is unlimited in principle in the cosmos. Another is that, in cases where inner material is pushing to emerge, its denial can have disastrous results, as in the loss of self-image that is so prevalent. As William Blake put it, "sooner murder an infant in its cradle than nurse unacted desires."[11] If we could let go of such desires, we would be all right, but as we "nurse" them, we grow bitter, and this bitterness comes out of us in one form or another.

The Unfolding

Our emergence, or the emergence of consciousness from within us as individuals, is analogous to the whole process of the evolution of consciousness out of the unconscious primordial stuff of the universe, described in the previous chapters. The universe "begins" as pure hydrogen, which is unconscious, though it is spirit-matter (see chapter 2). After about fifteen billion years of evolution (where the world is now), consciousness appeared on Earth as a phenomenon *drawn out of* the primordial matter, that is, spirit-matter, which has been complexified in cosmic processes.

But who or what "leads out?" Who or what draws forth consciousness out of spirit-matter? What is the source of that pull whose goal is the formation of personhood? In *Report to Greco*, author Nikos Kazantzakis described that something as "the Cry":

Blowing through heaven and earth, and in our hearts and the heart of every living thing, is a gigantic breath—a great Cry— which we call God. Plant life wished to continue its motionless sleep beside stagnant waters, but the Cry leaped up within it and violently shook its roots: "Away, let go of the earth, walk!" Had the tree been able to think and judge, it would have cried, "I don't want to. What are you urging me to do? You are demanding the impossible!" But the Cry, without pity, kept shaking its roots and shouting, "Away, let go of the earth, walk!" It shouted in this way for thousands of eons; and lo! as a result of desire and struggle, life escaped the motionless tree and was liberated.

Animals appeared—worms—making themselves at home in water and mud. "We're just fine here," they said. "We have peace and security; we're not budging!"

But the terrible Cry hammered itself pitilessly into their loins. "Leave the mud, stand up, give birth to your betters!" "We don't want to! We can't!" "You can't, but I can. Stand up!"

And lo! after thousands of eons, humankind emerged, trembling on still unsolid legs.

The human being is a centaur, with equine hoofs planted in the ground, but with body from breast to head worked on and tormented by the merciless Cry. The Cry has been fighting, again for thousands of eons, to draw itself, like a sword, out of its animalistic scabbard. It is also fighting—this is its new struggle—to draw itself out of this human scabbard. We call in despair, "Where can I go? I have reached the pinnacle, beyond is the abyss." And the Cry answers, "I am beyond. Stand up!"

All things are centaurs. It this were not the case, the world would rot into inertness and sterility.[12]

This image of the Cry suggests that becoming conscious is a process that attempts to draw humanity beyond itself and that is potentially endless. It also reflects a view in which there appear numerous steps that could be called "saving," as the threshold of each new freedom meets the inertia of being-as-it-now-is. In each step, the Cry itself is liberated, is saved, but its carriers can also be said to be saved. Kazantzakis certainly portrays humanity in need of a step that it has not yet taken. The evolution of world mythology has also portrayed these stages of saving humanity from the night-world of its unconscious roots.

In ancient Egypt, the bringer of culture (music, ritual, agriculture, literature, science) was the god Osiris, who on that account was designated "savior." In *Religion in Essence and Manifestation*, historian of religions Gerardus van der Leeuw summarizes the idea of salvation as ongoing potency, which has taken forms such as that of water for agriculture, of fire for the power of civilization, of spring in the seasonal cycle, and particularly of offspring for the continuance of life and of the accumulated knowledge of humanity. In ancient times, the son had special significance as, for example, Horus, the son of Osiris, who was the protector and sustainer of his father. Other examples are abundant. Van der Leeuw stresses that

> *God . . . is a late comer in the history of religion. And the remarkable thing is that . . . God the son subsisted before God the father; the savior is thus a primeval form subsisting side by side with that of the mother.*[13]

The offspring carries a new will, which preserves traditional values but is not bound to or limited by them as was the parent. It sees that which is newly emergent as something to be valued and struggles to integrate that with what already exists. In the general view of human history, this is salvation, and it is not difficult to see that the Christ of Christian mythology fits this pattern exactly, in those texts (mostly in the gospel of John) that bear upon the matter. "I and the father are one," taken with "behold I make all things new," is one obvious case.[14]

Finally, the cosmos itself draws us forth in the great unfolding. It is a world of mystery, majesty, and beauty, even when one must dig deeply to see it. As poet W. H. Auden put it,

> *The Garden is the only place there is, but you will not find it Until you have searched for it everywhere, and found no place that is not a desert.*[15]

In the end, the curious kitten is more important cosmologically than we at first supposed. It is most remarkable, and indispensable to evolution, that we are drawn out into the world. The kitten's explorations show this clearly at a prehuman level. We might say that the element of play is evident, as it also is in the often lethal tussles that the offspring of bipedal vertebrates get into. Play is of the same essence as exploration and is often the medium of our problem-solving activities. That which is unpredictable is permitted, and then the field leads us to the sought-after solution to a puzzle. It is a short step from the concept of the cosmos as play to the cosmos as dance. This view is enhanced by the tremendous wealth of ritual that surrounds play as well, in such ideas as what is "fair."

Playing is something we do with a surplus of energy, or with energy in excess of what is needed for mere subsistence. But culture, including our various forms of play, does not merely afford us a way of "working off" otherwise useless energy. Rather, we discover that culture feeds our souls in ways in which we might not have thought we needed nourishment. The evolution of religion, I feel, also serves inner needs humanity as a whole has not yet acknowledged in full consciousness, as witnessed by the quotation from Steven Weinberg above. Many humans know the need for nourishment in that area very deeply, but others see it as a sort of shameful legacy from the past, rather than as an opening to fuller human living.

Unfolding Energy

The fact that we possess an organic structure that provides us with surplus energy manifests a general property of life in the cosmos. That surplus allows us to go beyond physical nourishment to cultural nourishment, and beyond that to what we are now in process of pulling out from its cultural scabbard, namely, the religious dimension. As we discover these other sources of energy, psychic and spiritual, we find that each yields a surplus that we can integrate into our living. Something is drawing us out ever further into the realm of spirituality.

It seems as if surplus energy is supplied, as it were, from "below" (physiologically) and from "above" (spiritually, from the spiritual side of the patterned field, via a symbol) at the same time. The as-from-above aspect is the being-led-out, being attracted to creation and its spiritual beauties. Like a rope that is pushed from one end, however, it folds and goes this way and that. At least that is how our present spiritual explorations seem to me when I look at the planet as a whole. It seems that the element of choice needs much fuller development in relation to the use of our surplus energy. This development can come, as noted earlier, by permitting the opposites to come to consciousness within ourselves and struggling to evolve our personal values in the process of reconciling them.

It is as if the person-aspect of the Patterning, in whatever constituted the "decision" to embody, to create a cosmos as a place of finite being, "foresaw" (with the divine heart) this need for attractiveness in order that he/she would be drawn out from within and not be forever lost in material inertness. This emergence of God, involving the unfolding of spiritual energy, is something I feel is now moving in the mythic dimension. We will explore it in the next two chapters. It is also something very natural, something to be expected now that we have begun to transcend rationalism.

We may use a visualization to illustrate the viewpoint being developed here. Picture yourself as a potential visitor to Earth from some other planet. Your ship pauses high above the night side of Earth, and you look at the diffuse glow from urban concentrations below. You might have the thought: Ah! nature has taken its course here: after a planet has been around for so long, a glow appears on its surface representing the gathering and concentration of energy. You would be correct: the gathering and concentration *is* a universal property of nature. We are merely nature's agents in the process.

If you hold together in your mind the light that has appeared on the surface of the planet with the darkness on the night side of a planet in the early stages of the evolution of life, perhaps you can feel a sense of reconnection of spirit with the material aspect of nature out of which it has been born. Even though you realize that the light is produced by beings on the surface, who must have passed a certain threshold on the way to consciousness, you pause to reflect on the tendency of light to emerge on a planet, for life to concentrate and focus itself in this manner, gathering energy. It is extremely satisfying, in part because you have come all the way here as an explorer yourself, but partly because of the sheer beauty of the light, which is pure nature in a living cosmos. However complex the process, *light happens.*

It is as if one first encountered a honeycomb and did not know of the agency of the bees in building this elegant wax structure and in gathering this extraordinary stuff that fills it. You just might say, "Ah! Honey happens."

Indeed, the human agency in gathering energy has often been regarded as nearly as automatic as that of bees making honey: humans gather energy, or rather, *life* gathers energy. It is only later that one discovers the phenomenon of "interestedness," which, at various stages of evolution, was essential to life's progress. Of course, interest is a judgment from hindsight, but there is this exploratory something in nature, which I call God-wanting-to-come-out, wanting, as it were, to reach the light—the light of consciousness. We really are in the process of "letting the (curious) kitten out of the bag."

As we get closer to viewing this coming-out quality as a phenomenon of nature, we are more able to see it as an aspect of the cosmos as a whole. The Anthropic Principle says that, if we are here, it is because of a property of the cosmos which not only permits but also ensures that something of our kind, with all of our own characteristics, will occur.

That same property of the cosmos is already at work to ensure that the posthuman emergence will happen as well.

CHAPTER 4

Godding

Understand that thou hast within thyself herds of cattle, flocks of sheep, and flocks of goats. Understand that the fowls of the air are also within thee. Understand that thou thyself art another world in little, and hast within thee the sun and the moon, and also the stars.

—ORIGEN, "Homily on Leviticus"

There is nothing outside us that does not belong inside—even God.[1] In order to make such a statement meaningful, I need to gather here (in a substantial part of this chapter) something of what I feel the word *God* means as regards the physical cosmos, though I hope the meaning of that term will continue to grow throughout the book. We tend to "see" God as external and have even felt it as blasphemous to think of God as within ourselves as well, though the idea has had a long and fertile history within Christianity, to name just one religion. On the other hand, we have seen nature as manifesting the grandeur of God, even making God somehow visible.

The "divine" qualities that follow are intended to show some ways in which God is visible, in the sense just given, and to make it easier to visualize what "taking God within" might mean, that is, if we were to find ways to assimilate these qualities into our way of being and living.

The idea of assimilating God is not at all new. It is at least hinted in many religions, such as the Hindu practice of "awakening the Kundalini serpent" and thus bringing life to the divine centers within us. My intent, however, is to be less mystical.

Aspects of God in the Cosmos

1. *Purposiveness.* The first essential aspect of God comes from a sense that there is purposiveness in evolution. I have used this word before without explanation, but I should say here that the difference between purposiveness and, say, directionality is that the former has a face (see the prologue), while the latter does not. When we say that God is purposive, we are saying that something is happening that seems to be unfolding a world of meaning. One way that scientists refer to this sense of purposiveness is through the concept of a "fine-tuned" universe, which provides the physical basis for the "cosmic ecology" to be presented in chapter 6. For instance, the relative strengths, as well as the precise nature, of the various physical forces must be exactly what they are to sustain both stars and living forms. That is, balancing is required for stars and living forms to both be included in one cosmos. The relationships upon which the total balance depends are quite numerous. For example, the lifetimes of the stars that form planets are long enough for life to evolve on the planets, while the lifetimes of stars that do not form planets are shorter, and those latter stars explode and enrich the process of star formation with heavy elements out of which planets are made. This is just one complex relationship depending on the relative strengths of the forces. The facts that water exists in a liquid form and can be a medium to contain evolving life and that the molecular bonds formed by carbon can make long chains of atoms of infinite variety also fit together to foster life in an amazingly precise way. Physicist Freeman Dyson suggests that "there is a peculiar harmony

between the structure of the universe and the needs of life and intelligence."[2]

The sense of the cosmos as functioning purposively for the support of living beings must be expanded to include not only the evolution of consciousness but also the most profound spiritual aspirations of living beings. In the first chapter, I spoke of consciousness as grounded in organic living being, based on a "within," an interior quality that is present even in molecules. I generally use the word *consciousness* in the sense in which Jung used it, that of self-reflexive consciousness, as in the epigraph to chapter 1. Consciousness is something that evolution builds toward over billions of years but does not strictly exist until the ego emerges, although a deeper consciousness becomes available to us as we learn to be aware of the Self (again, see the prologue). All that is biologically alive is part of the great thrust of evolution, the fact that it tends to produce life, complexity, and subtlety. Every scaled, furry, or winged creature is integral to the whole and needed by that evolutionary movement. As a creature with an at least partially developed and filled within, it is part of God.

Some creatures also meditate on, and communicate with each other about, where the whole cosmos is going, and they try to discern what is behind it all. They study what they see, devise instruments to aid their seeing, and create a written memory to free their minds for deeper explorations.[3] Some of them also endanger themselves and the world in the adolescence of their intellectualism by separating themselves both intellectually and emotionally from the whole planet and all of its life-forms, but I do not want to dwell on that aspect of their lives here. The point is that everything that is taken inside from without increases our freedom to adapt to the world and to the cosmos.

If we feel, in the evident tendency of evolution to bring forth life, consciousness, and spirituality, that something is moving with purpose, we can use our feelings to give to that something a name that honors the integrative unity of the evolving cosmos: God. All ants, beetles, lizards, and serpents are part of that movement and that whole, and humans are as well. In this view, all are part of the whole being, and through our eyes and comprehension, God "sees" creation in this manner for the first time. This is not to say that God is not experiencing creation in two maple-beetles mating but only that a new form of seeing is made possible by the advent of ego-consciousness. A few million years from now, those of our descendants who are carrying the first flame of newer being will be much more deeply aware than we of the whole of creation and of what God desires for the integration of the cosmos and the fulfillment of the beings living in it. Their religious consciousness will be vastly different from our own.

2. *Life.* The second indication of God is a feeling for the power of life, as in Teilhard de Chardin's statement that "the universe is fundamentally and primarily *living.*" In the first chapter, I spoke to the fact that life has no beginning but only degrees of actualization. Every single atom carries the impetus to engender living beings. Here I am not fine-tuning the idea so much as I am stressing that life is part of the fundamental nature of things—and that that is why the cosmos is a nonrational complex of opposites.

In the first chapter, I also spoke of the fundamental disequilibrium of the cosmos, that everything in it must keep on evolving, as well as the fact that, through that continuing evolution, the cosmos poses problems for us that only love can solve. It is the power of life, the aliveness of the cosmos, to enter into situations and stir up those problems. These qualities actually derive from the nonrational relationship of opposites.[4] I have also described the roots of the fact that being fully aware as a human requires courage and, one might add, humor.

3. *Uniqueness.* Though I do feel that God patterns unique individuals, endows them with personhood, and can be related to personally by them, I cannot feel God as a being or a person. Without

being a person, God brings forth persons. A person is something finite, unlike God's own being, but finite personhood fulfills that being in a mysterious way. Perhaps we could call this third aspect of God "Person." I also speak of the "Face in the cosmos," or the "Heart of the cosmos," as qualities evoking person. Our notion of a person is so concrete that it is most difficult to find a word that suggests personness without being concrete. I will be consistent in using the singular (person) when referring to this aspect of God.

4. *The Patterning.* I call God by other names, too, especially the Patterning and the Omniscience. (If I use the same words without capitals I am referring to the concepts of omniscience and patterning, rather than specifically to God.) In chapter 1, I described the Patterning as a guiding field that shapes the development of life but which also includes that which we try to describe by means of our physical laws. I use *the Patterning* when referring to the fact that the cosmos is ordered and purposive and that it shapes evolutionary development of life and beings. I use *the Omniscience* when stressing the feeling of providence, the fact that, mysteriously, we meet with what we need for the sake of our consciousness, both individually and for the planet.

This is perhaps the moment to speak of a general aspect of my outlook that may help to clarify much in this chapter. I said just above that, without being a person, God brings forth persons. This is a general model for the emergence of finite, concrete, manifestations of qualities of the infinite. As persons are the finite manifestation of the God-quality of "person," so patterns are manifestations of the Patterning, and consciousness is a manifestation of Omniscience. This whole book is an attempt to account for the cosmos as a finite manifestation of the infinite Source of all that is. We need very much to be clear about the notion that there is something that God "wants" in all this, that is, in the movement from the infinite to the finite, in the embodiment of spirit.

Unlike Buddhists, I generally use the word *desire* for

something positive, not egocentric (which I would tend to call *craving* instead). Our own deepest "heart's desire" for union with the Divine is not at all egocentric but is in keeping with God's desire for union with finitude. This unity is something that one both has and has not at the same time. What we have is the infinite root or archetype that ever moves us toward deeper union as it can; what we lack is the possibility of a final concrete finite manifestation. But let us return to the God-aspects of the cosmos.

One aspect of the Patterning that I find especially moving is the fact that freedom is built into the way in which the Patterning produces finite existence. For freedom to be real, every situation must offer us a choice of what we will value on the one hand and on the other sufficient free energy or will to weigh the positive and negative aspects of our choices and to choose among them. Because everything that comes to being embodies nonrational opposites, the presence of options is guaranteed in physical becoming. Physical reality is nondeterministic. Of course, we have personal psychological structures that often make the options inaccessible to us for the time being; but means of opening ourselves do exist, especially by gaining exposure to more and more experience beyond our immediate surroundings, that is, by going out of, or beyond, ourselves, which is the same as taking more of the world into our being. The encountered facts that tend to break down our psychic "walls" also tend to release enough energy for choice in the process.

The Patterning is also transformative, as an aspect of the fundamental disequilibrium of the cosmos and of life. It keeps infolding or involuting through level upon level of being. (I am only describing these qualities here briefly; they are expanded elsewhere.)[5]

5. *Omniscience.* As I have said, omniscience is to be distinguished from consciousness. Jung defines consciousness as the relationship of psychic contents to an ego.[6] The term *contents* is just

a general reference to anything of which I, the ego, could possibly be aware. I am aware of, conscious of, things in my physical environment, knowledge of things which I have learned, certain tendencies in my behavior, situations that might give me anxiety or humor, feelings for others, or for what I intend to do today or in the long run. All of these are examples of contents. Their defining element is that they are in my consciousness once they are related to my ego, so that I am aware of them. If I decide to recall some places I have been, and an image of one of those places comes into my awareness, it is an item of content that was unconscious the moment before but has come to consciousness in the process of recollection. This mode of operation makes consciousness finite and specific.

I must use caution in speaking of the ego, since for some people the word *ego* has only a negative connotation. The qualities of the ego that can be negative I refer to as *egocentricity*. The ego itself is merely the observer in us who sees and thinks by means of contrasts. It is also the "I" who can learn to make choices in relation to values beyond itself. The very real possibility of egocentricity is a necessary danger, since God needs our egos for the sake of freedom, creativity, and love, as pointed out above.

An ego becomes aware of things by means of contrasts (figure and ground) rather than through an undifferentiated flow of contents through the mind. It can only become aware of one thing in terms of its difference from another.

Often our consciousness is able to hold awareness of only one opposite, as figure and ground sometimes can change into one another. But as we become more aware of the opposites that inhere not only in each situation of living but also in each element of consciousness, it becomes apparent that even our sharpest figure/ground distinctions are partial, and even our contrast-knowledge brings the field with it in the concrete object.[7] The deeper our consciousness is, the more we are aware of the ultimate inseparability of opposites in our lives or the inadequacy of pure intellect to comprehend reality.

The heart of this life of ours is neither rational nor representable, because opposites cannot be represented simultaneously as held together in the same thing.[8] The closest we come to representation of something holding opposites (which Jung calls the "transcendent function"), is by means of symbols that can hold for us the experience of the *numinous,* of which Rudolf Otto spoke in *The Idea of the Holy.*[9] Otto used the expression *mysterium tremendum* to hold the two principal opposites that describe the numinous: *mysterium* conveying a more quiet ineffability and *tremendum* conveying the majesty and glory, the sheer magnitude of God in relation to such tiny creatures as ourselves.

The Patterning is much more than the shaping of evolution and the development of complex organic forms as containers of life, consciousness, and spirituality. The field is the web that puts in our path what we need in our lives as individuals. That is, it operates in particulars, but unconsciously, since God as creator, not being a being, has no ego. Since some people have an idea of the unconscious as chaotic, I feel it important to approach this point, too, with some caution. To me it seems the very opposite. God's "knowing" is nonrational field-knowledge, while we know (in ego-consciousness) by means of contrasts of figure and ground.[10] The field also affects us, and we can learn to discern its operation in our lives. True consciousness or awakening becomes possible for us when we can function from field-knowledge as well as from contrast-knowledge, or what is the same thing, from the Self (the inner God-image) as well as from the ego.

I have spoken of the richness of creation that comes into being under the Patterning. This does not mean that God must think specific thoughts for each water molecule that freezes into the pattern of each snowflake. Nor is God some kind of "number-crunching" computer. Things must be patterned in a different manner, one that *remains intrinsic to the phenomenon that is happening,* while maintaining an intimate connection to the "heart of the universe," which is the same as all of the aspects of God I have been describing, taken together. They "add up" to a *loving* God. *It is my conviction that the Omniscience is unconscious under the definition given above.* That is, I will distinguish between God-as-creator, the prior being (again, not *a* being), possessing no ego-consciousness, the unconscious Patterning; and God-as-internalized, who/which comes to fullness in evolution (never complete) by means of our egos (and those of other sentient creatures in the cosmos) when we choose commitment to do the God's will. Then the Omniscience is the name for the overall unconscious knowledge in the field.

6. *Freedom.* I take the Patterning as the source of all that is, in all of its paradoxicality and freedom. Freedom is grounded in opposites, for without opposites there would be no possibility of choice. For us, there is no possibility of choice without the consciousness of the opposites between which to choose. This shows, as clearly as anything can, the relationship of freedom and consciousness. The Worldfield is the ultimate complex of opposites and therefore the ultimate presenter of choices, for whom all things are possible in a patterned way. But the Patterning works toward ever more consciousness, ever more freedom, ever more choicefulness (the essential expression of freedom) in creatures. Since we find ourselves face to face, as it were, with this situation, which seems to engage us with an apparent intelligence, we may also use the term *God* for this presenter.

I believe that the freedom that comes to actualization in finite beings is the ultimate meaning of the freedom *of God,* and is the final purpose of the Godding, the process by which true consciousness develops out of the cosmos. Here a friend says, "But isn't it true that, in many, God's freedom has been assassinated?" Indeed it is, both by ourselves and by others, but God takes that risk with us out of love.

As symbols of the Divine to complete the list of what I mean by God-aspects of the cosmos, I want to mention music, for it represents to us concretely the effect of the Patterning upon living beings: it is both outside us and within and links the inner and outer in a unique manner. It moves us both physically and spiritually. As sound, it is truly nonrational and symbolizes the field (see chapter 1). Insofar as we can understand or analyze it (and understanding of music is always partial and changeable), music shows us how contrast-knowledge is slowly coagulated out of the field, for, in spite of its concreteness and reproducibility, music resists contrast-analysis. This is true of visual art as well. The fact that we find beauty is noteworthy in itself, because our sense of beauty is the clue to meaning. It satisfies our spirituality in a profound way. It can be simplicity or complexity, darkness or light, or the holding of opposites together. What we find to be beautiful is a measure of our depth and openness. When we experience art, we come close to the Patterning consciously; but the Patterning affects our lives unconsciously at all times.

The Godding

There is nothing outside us that does not belong inside. We spend so much of our life's energy being cautious and building defenses, holding the world at bay. If we could risk more of an opening of ourselves to living and to other beings, we might experience more pain, but we certainly would experience more joy. Some things easily evoke a positive inner response. These are the safe things, or those of obvious beauty. Other things evoke revulsion and are not easily accepted as parts of ourselves, or even as parts of God's world. These things reside in what Jung called our shadow, but they are not the only contents there. We also fear the greatness within each of us, which is a fact very much to the point of the present chapter.

One of the things that could help us to overcome our fears is remembering that our ego is only a small part of our total selves. Similarly, we need to remember that the visible personality of others (even if they are not operating merely from a persona) is still only a minor part of their total being. We hide from others, as well as from ourselves, both our wounds and our potentials. Sometimes it takes a profound personal disaster to open us up to the realities behind the human interactions in which we participate. A friend of mine, dying of cancer, said, "Why does it take this for us to speak to each other of our love?" He was not referring to the two of us but rather to the general fact that we live such closed lives.

The major transformations of our lives are openings, often painful ones, that increase our acceptance of others and of ourselves. Usually we have to learn that we are neither as wise nor as good as we had hoped and that the traits of others that seemed reprehensible to us are not so unlike our own. This is one aspect of life, seen as a journey of discovery.

The "visionary journey," as described by psychologist Marie-Louise von Franz on the basis of the work of Henri Corbin, "leads to a *continuing and progressive internalization* of the whole cosmos."[11] For the sake of what we call humility, God is the last thing we would speak of to others, of all the things outside that belong inside. But the topic of this chapter, Godding, is exactly that, the gradual and progressive internalization of God. The process might also be called the inner awakening of God, which reflects the human awakening to the divine presence within. To the degree that this process is actualized in any of us, we might speak of God-as-Godded.

I view this whole process as God the creator giving birth to God-as-Godded *through us* (and other creatures in the cosmos) and emphatically *not* as us, on our own, giving birth to God. The fact that we also have life as individuals with infinite potential for fulfillment is a bonus. Thus I speak both of our awakening to the divine presence within and the awakening of God within us. *In the Godding process, God makes use of our ego-consciousness when and to the extent that we can transcend our ego-bound intentions and permit the gift of God to shape our will to the values in the universe.* We are then co-creators of the fulfilling life, for only consciousness enables freedom. God needs our commitment but cannot force it without negating the freedom that is its goal. Thus, the divine experiment on any given planet is a risk and could fail.

Author Virginia Mollenkott, in her book *Godding*, gives her conception of Godding as a "mirroring" of divine attributes, such as unconditional love, that preserves the individual's discreteness and distance from God. She does call it an "embodiment," and quotes Blake's lines: "Where Mercy, Love, and Pity dwell, / There God is dwelling too."[12] Many of the questions with which she deals are specific to Christianity, but she does include the darkness of God as part of the "Ground of our Being and Becoming."[13] She also says, "All of us are invited to devote ourselves to the lifestyle of godding."[14] Perhaps the word *lifestyle* is a bit unfortunate, for it conveys the sense of something that we try out or put on. The image of Godding that I am attempting to describe is anything but a lifestyle. Rather, it is *the living of one's true heart from within, fulfilling the intention of God for our being.*

I want to say very clearly that God does not awaken within the ego but within the person. One way in which Jung develops this notion is to describe it as that of a more comprehensive personality emerging from within and taking the ego into its service. But this cannot happen unless the ego sacrifices its claim to be master in the house. Paradoxically, the sacrifice is meaningless unless the ego first possesses itself, i.e., is indeed its own master in a profound sense. By this I refer to a personal integrity in depth and a personality that has learned openness by daring to cross boundaries. Like Jesus when he said, "If possible, let this cup [crucifixion] pass from me," self-possessed persons know their own desires.[15] Only a sacrifice of something that is of great value to oneself can be valuable to God, whether it be the "widow's mite"[16] or the egocentric control of our lives. The sacrifice is epitomized by Jesus' statement in the same passage, "Not my will but thine be done." Paradoxically, in giving over his will to God, Jesus did not lose his self-possession. This was by no means the first time that Jesus had committed his will to God. That was the very stuff of his life, from at least the time that he sought out John to receive the baptism signifying repentance.

There are many paradoxes involved in establishing a relationship with God through the Self.[17] For example, like everyone else when young, I felt that I was I throughout my whole life, from infancy on, though there was not even an "I" in infancy. In adolescence, too, the ego struggles to establish its identity and independence, not knowing that other awakenings will occur. Sometime around age thirty, I, again as with many others, awakened to the notion that my previous ego was by no means my true being, and I began to search for that being, only to learn after much journeying that it had been with me and guiding me and repressed by me all along. I was not the "prime inhabitant" of my person but only the bearer of my limited contrast-knowledge. This "I" was a continually changing something; but within (beyond the within of the ego), there was a source of continuity that linked the givens of my birth with the potential fulfillment of my present being. When the ego's transformations reach this point, there is at last the potential for a true sacrifice of ego-will. There need be no hubris associated with the ego letting go of its ego-will and entering into a living relationship with the Prime Inhabitant.

In her study *Puer Aeternus*, von Franz stresses that, in the meeting of ego and Self, both are wounded—the ego in that it must give up control and the Self in that it must give up eternal possibility and become actualized in a concrete waking life.[18] This is an image that fits the Navajo myth of the blind and crippled twins, the blind one carrying the crippled one and the crippled one giving guidance on their journey.

Prior to a time about a decade ago, I would not have spoken in terms of Godding but would have stuck to the Jungian terminology of the relationship of ego and Self and the integrative process of "individuation." Jung used cautious, scientific language, masking his deep concern for God, which he finally revealed both in his *Memories, Dreams, Reflections* and in *Answer to Job*.[19]

My primary insight came in the reading of *Answer to Job*. Many who have read this book have experienced it as explosive, but shocking language can sometimes stimulate an awakening. The book of Job, on which *Answer to Job* is based, attempts to give a possible background for God's testing of our faith through personal disasters. We usually speak of such disasters as befell Job in the story as incomprehensible. However, Jung insisted that we must look at God through the eyes of *our own* moral standards, that is, we must *remain ourselves* and not forfeit our moral consciousness in order to excuse God. To Jung, God's "behavior" as portrayed in Job is not incomprehensible but reprehensible, and only excusable on the grounds of God's unconsciousness. Jung did not accuse God either of playing "dirty tricks" on Job or of "testing" Job, but rather of an "amorality" that is best described as unconsciousness.

When Job's response to God in the book is seen in this light, we find that Job's human consciousness held a value that God lacked, especially *in the recognition that his persecutor is also his redeemer* (holding the opposites in his awareness simultaneously). Job "holds fast" to his integrity in the knowledge that he has not sinned, and God praises this steadfastness in the end, adding that Job's "friends," in accusing him of some hidden fault, had not "said what was right." In understanding this material and in speaking of what God lacks, we need to remember what was mentioned above concerning the desire of the Infinite for finite manifestation. Morality is a desire in God, a part of the Patterning, which takes form in humans, but only concrete contrast-consciousness provides the footholds for choice.

Disasters befall us not because of our having "sinned" (in the common sense of specific misdeeds or omissions) but because God needs awakening. Jesus also gave a parable of a sleeping God who will only give us the bread we need if *persistently importuned* (Luke 11:5–8, which follows immediately after "Give us this day our daily bread"). The question of why evil can happen to a good person is thus answered in a way most of us find difficult to hear or to ingest: God is unconscious and needs our finite contrast-consciousness. Otherwise, there is only omniscience, which does not become concrete until physical organic beings evolve with enough complexity in their nervous systems for self-reflexivity. Does this mean that God does not "know right from wrong?" In the case of Job, apparently so, although our moral consciousness derives from the Patterning, so at least the potential for right moral choice is there.

We are derived from God, and we complete creation via the attainment of consciousness. Only insofar as *we* know does *God* know in finitude as well as in Omniscience, and only insofar as we act on a moral basis does God act concretely, for moral distinctions are a function of consciousness. When we desire justice and act for it, we fulfill God's inherent desire for justice, and the Godding takes a step.

The insight came to me where Jung says the following concerning God's tremendous show of power to Job, speaking in the voice out of the whirlwind, as part of the first response just mentioned:

> *So even in Job's day Yahweh is still intoxicated with the tremendous power and grandeur of [God's] creation. Compared with this, what are Satan's pinpricks and the lamentations of human beings . . . even if they do bear God's image? Yahweh seems to have forgotten this fact entirely, otherwise [Yahweh] would never have ridden so roughshod over Job's human dignity.*[20]

Part of present human consciousness, represented by Job, manifests a new integrity, but part still manifests the earlier unconscious deity. It is human beings who are clearly intoxicated with the tremendous power and grandeur of creation. This has been expressed clearly by scientists and others who have been closely involved with the creation and possible use of nuclear devices. Some voiced the feeling of holding God's power in their hands and also either having the control over it or releasing it violently on command. It is human beings who act out the God who first responded to Job by riding roughshod over the dignity of other humans, sometimes in God's name, which, in the view of Godding, *is precisely the same thing as God doing it.* A difficulty lies in the fact that, since God shows the tendencies manifest in the symbolic case of Job, we can also deliver God's wrath as well as love. Only by becoming more conscious and acting morally can we help God's love overcome God's wrath, as suggested by a divine prayer in the Midrash, "May it be my will that my love overcome my wrath."[21]

Our conscious or unconscious actions can tip the balance either way.

Since the needs of justice and mercy come into conflict as humans actually go about living, both of these divine desires can only be reconciled in particular concrete situations. In the end, we live out the will of God not by "knowing right from wrong" but by weighing values with love.

Jung also feels that portrayals of God in human myth and scripture show an evolution of divine consciousness at the same time as they manifest the evolution of human consciousness. For him, the "answer to Job" is the incarnation of Christ, for Job's integrity was a concrete step toward bringing the Self inside the human, which builds the strength of the inner God-image and reduces the tendency to project it. The light of consciousness that Yahweh felt in Job was such a challenge that the first divine response was the parading of divine power before the helpless human, Job, but the second response was a divine resolve to become fully human. Jesus took a tremendous step in this direction, in consequence of which the divinity shining within him has been recognized as paradigmatic. But the process of taking God inside can never be complete in any finite individual and will continue as long as the cosmos sustains planets.

In the evolution of moral consciousness, we begin to see the effect of God's becoming human in a greater manifestation of positive divine qualities on the part of humans. The love that we are able to put into action towards our neighbors, as towards ourselves, is God's love from within ourselves. This is the essence of Godding. But unless it can find concrete living through us, the comprehensive personality mentioned above, the Self, retains the eternal, unconscious, and ruthless aspect of older God-concepts. (We speak of this older form of God when we say that some disaster has "befallen us.") God needs us precisely for our capacity for moral reflection.

Nonetheless, the past twenty-five hundred years have seen steady growth in our human consciousness of the Self, the representative of God within humanity, and of our ability to relate to it and to relate from it to others. Relating to others and to the earth from the Self is a concrete image of the Godding. In the next chapter, we will fill out the picture of how humans can participate in this divine process.

However, this seems to be a place to say again why the heart-vision of the cosmos becomes the primary vision, once it is taken up. In view of the Godding, it is simply that issues of living are the primary ones in our lives, and how we live determines everything that brightens or darkens our humanity, as well as whether we will continue as a species, evolving toward something greater than we now are.

CHAPTER 5

Awakening

*Who goes to dine must take his feast
Or find the banquet mean—
The Table is not laid without
Till it is laid within.*
—EMILY DICKINSON

*O, the eyes of God watch out of
each one of us.*
—KENNETH PATCHEN, Sleepers Awake

Awakening is a property of the cosmos. This chapter shows how we awaken psychologically and how our awakening becomes God's awakening.

The previous chapter described a number of qualities of the physical cosmos that seem to indicate a divine presence. It also defined "the Godding," which is not only the awakening of the Divine within each of us but a process wherein we are assimilated to the work of God in the ongoing evolution of the earth and awaken to that work. If such is our destiny, or that of our offspring, it is a great one indeed. It takes courage, to start with, and a real development of understanding both of our nature and the nature of the cosmos in which we live. It is not an exercise of the mind but of the total being, which is part of why we must now revision the cosmos (and ourselves) with the heart.

Coming to Be in the Cosmos

In the Big Bang, the birth of our cosmos, the "stuff of the universe" was precipitated out of the cosmic field into concrete being, the whole cosmos coming to existence in an instant, with the divine attributes described in the previous chapter. I will describe this process more fully in another chapter. Here I only want to make use of the image of something emerging or falling out of the field into concrete being.

Our own personal coming to be occurs in a process that is parallel to this and that is also a precipitation out of the field, just as the infant emerges out of the womb. There is preparation and process in the field, in the womb that is the cosmos of the infant. Even as adults we still share the total interconnectedness of the field, even in our finitude and our separateness, our having been born. At our inner center, we are connected to everything that is seen as "outside."

The Big Bang brought to birth a patterned yet unformed (undifferentiated) stuff that evolved into galaxies, stars, and planets. Once planets were formed, the stuff on their surfaces evolved a part of itself into living beings, which underwent a continual transformation into more and more complex forms. In a similar manner, the baby's birth brings forth a patterned, undeveloped being with potentiality for aliveness, consciousness, and spiritual transformation.

The infant's consciousness is completely unformed, though the behavior is patterned. Neither "I" nor "not-I" has come to being, and it behaves in accordance with what psychologists call "infantile omnipotence." It cries and its needs are met; the "world" is at its service, as far as it can tell. If the world never says "No," the infant will never have to revise its views of reality. We also describe this state as being identified with the universe or as the "archaic identity of subject and object." I have included an appendix that elaborates this concept but will give a brief view of it here.

We project what is inside ourselves onto our surroundings, which gives us a false sense that we know how things work "out there." As we learn, we discover that our knowledge had been incomplete or erroneous. In most cases involving external facts, we can be corrected and go on from there, but not in all of these and especially not where values learned in childhood are concerned. *Where we are unaware of what we are projecting, we are unaware of ourselves.* When we learn of our projections, we learn of ourselves as well. In particular, we learn that we were mistaken about something, so that the process of recollection of our projections teaches us humility. We can be quite sure that we do not know everything about ourselves because we are certain that we do not know everything about the universe and its values. There is always some case where we are erroneously assuming (projecting) something about the way things are, and we are quite wrong! Even when scientists make some profound discovery, they say, "Oh! So *that* is how it is." This reestablishes the archaic identity, for we assume that present knowledge is final knowledge, though we have seen the fundamental physical worldview change enough to know better.

Though archaic identity is quite noticeable in groups that have not been exposed to the highly differentiated worldview of what we call modern nations and though in less differentiated cultures it forms the basis of animism (in which inner movements of psyche are experienced as spirits "out there"), we need to remain humble ourselves, for the errors we are currently making, whatever they are, could have potentially disastrous consequences. The more complex our societies, the more it is incumbent upon us to be open to learn of the universe. As I stressed in chapter 1, we are far from carrying through even our concrete knowledge of evolution in the way we live. If we did so, we would be required to revise the policies that exploit energy and physical resources, not to mention correcting the inhumanity of our political arrangements.[1]

From the original condition of identity with everything, the individual human becomes itself through a process of *taking inside and owning* all those things that belong to its individuality, properties with which it had previously endowed the environment of people and things. It also recognizes those things that are objectively other as "not-I." We become differentiated (individuated) by assimilating the contents of our own unconscious. That is, we reclaim or recollect ourselves from all that we have projected of our own unconscious onto the objects in the environment and become clearer as to what is truly out there or what is "other."

As the "not-I" takes form, the "I" takes form as well. We say we have learned about the world, but we equally have learned about ourselves. Much of what a child learns concerning the nature of reality comes through teaching rather than discovery. Some of it works well enough as long as one does not go beyond the nurture of the immediate group but proves inadequate when tested in wider experience. Other acquired knowledge proves well-founded with respect to all the experiences we are likely to have on this planet. But where a child gets its initial knowledge is tremendously important, for it is assimilated preconsciously and is among the most difficult worldview elements to transform.

Part of what a growing personality takes inside comes in personal discoveries, and part is whatever knowledge family, group, or society feels it good to impart. For the moment, I want only to bring in one such idea—one with which I have had the deepest struggles.

Interlude: Freedom versus the Apocalyptic View

Most adults believe the world is flawed. As a result, many religions try to address human problems from that perspective. One of these attempts is apocalypticism, the idea that, while things are indeed bad now, God will enter into the physical world at some time and effect a complete change of its nature such that the problems we now experience will become impossible. Apocalypticism expects sudden miraculous change, brought about by an external power. It would be difficult to count the times that I have longed not to have to slog through difficulties and imagined all sorts of miraculous scenarios that might turn aside the charging bull, so to speak, so that I would not have to face the realities confronting me. We might not actually defend, when pressed, the notion that God will change the world for our sakes, but I would wager that, when we are alone, many of us resort to apocalyptic fantasies. Since the problems we wish we could avoid arise in the conflicts that are the ground of human freedom, *this freedom would have to be eradicated in an apocalyptic transformation of the world.*

Since these also are the problems to be solved by means of love, we would forfeit that as well. We would fail to realize the love that we would experience in solving the problems.

Interlude Continued: Freedom and Love

The redemption of the state of the world, which is not the elimination of problems but the embodiment of love in concrete situations, will not take the form of making the world "all sweetness and light" apocalyptically. Only *love* could conceive a cosmos that ensures the freedom of its creatures, for to love *is* to set free. There are times when we will act to restrain a loved one from extreme self-destructiveness, but love desires not to control another. Rather, love seeks the unfolding of the other in all uniqueness.

Does God give us the freedom to choose? Our freedom, as I said in the previous chapter, exists to the degree that we are conscious, as does our power to love from inside. We may have more or less consciousness, but it is incumbent upon us to use what we have of both freedom and love.

We might begin by recognizing that we are free to interpret any statement as either loving or cynical and try to hold to our love before jumping to the defensive. Someone may say something hurtful to us, and we are free to assume that it was intended as such or that it comes from a wound and may actually be a cry for help or for love.

What will maximize love in a relationship? Do we demand that someone fill our needs as a price for feeling good about them, or do we simply attempt to help bring forth the true heart of the other because a human being is beautiful? In all this freedom, which of the options we have just examined feels most like the Godding? It is in us to stop slamming the door on that process.

In order to maximize the presence of love, however, our cosmos must hold to its problematic character. It must set problems that only *embodied love* can solve. Do we not yet see that what gives us the greatest feeling for humanity comes from our knowledge of human reactions to extreme conditions? By extreme conditions, I am referring to such as Jacques Lusseyran dealt with in the Buchenwald concentration camp, as described in the prologue. Since most of our tribulations cannot compare with these, let us see what we can do with what we do encounter.

A Cosmic Pawn Shop

If redemption is Godding—the joining of the ego and the Self in what Paul called a "new creation," or new being—this new being to which we are called is more comprehensive, more integrated, more whole.[2] It is also more specific and individual. Here we can only note that great personalities, such as Jesus, Moses, Confucius, and Buddha, were highly individual personalities. This picture is enhanced by including in our view other great ones from all over the world. Those who have contributed to our understanding of God have not necessarily been morally "pure," either.

Conventional moral views and behavior are not a prerequisite for transmitting God to others. What these and other great ones share is holding opposites together in their lives, being open to the Divine or listening to the inner voice and knowing themselves.

Von Franz quotes a wonderful passage from a Gnostic sect scripture called "The Gospel of Eve":

> *The prophetess sees God and hears him say: "I am thou, and thou art I, and wherever thou art, there am I, and I am scattered in all things, and from wherever thou wilt thou canst gather me, but in gathering me thou gatherest thyself."*[3]

This is a uniquely clear statement of the Godding, though it leaves out the aspect of sacrifice of ego-bound desires mentioned earlier.

The curious, common use of the word *redemption*, as in repaying borrowed cash to "redeem" some personal item, say, from a pawn shop, suggests the wonderful image of the whole cosmos as pawn shop. We look out among the stars and see, hanging there on little hooks in dark corners, pieces of our own existence, which are also parts of our God-being. On each is a date of loan and price tag, a promise that something of our own is there for us, when we gain the wherewithal to claim it.

Of course, our more immediate environment is full of the unredeemed pawn of God-in-us, from the shantytowns of the poor and oppressed throughout the world, to the homeless of our cities, and to even the "neighbors" with whom we interact every day without necessarily taking God-within-*them* into account. I must be very clear that it is not the people of these places who are unredeemed but *the parts of ourselves that dwell among them.* What I mean here is an expansion of the poetic image that "no one is an island." If someone dies, a piece of me dies also but not just with the neighbors of my immediate environment. It is impossible for individual humans to take all other individual humans on Earth into their hearts. It would be heroic enough if we simply took a moment to let the death of others in trouble spots of the world have an impact upon us even briefly, with the realization that something of us is no more. We should be able to empathize with large segments of humanity, but it is also important that some individual also moves us daily *to an awareness of the unity of humanity, including ourselves* as well. I suspect that we are fearful of the part of our hearts that would respond.

Does God wait to be discovered? What else can a loving God do, who desires the freedom of the created? God must wait, like Sleeping Beauty for the kiss. When I meditate on the billions of years from the Big Bang to the first emergence of consciousness, I have a profound sense of God waiting. And then there is all that will come to life in the billions of years to come. Most of God is still hidden and waiting. Yet there is a sympathy of all life that flows through the whole evolutionary process, even in the cataclysm of an exploding star. If God is in all things of the cosmos, then only as we unify the cosmos, that is, as we assimilate the unity of the cosmos in our own beings, will we really build God's concrete reality.[4] I say "we" but only in the sense indicated above, of cooperation of the human with the Divine in mutual sacrifice and fulfillment.

Can we speak of the redemption of God? The image I get from this question is that of God lying fallow and hidden in "fields" all over the earth. So much of God goes unused and unactivated on a given day and calls precisely for redemption. Where will we find God? In a stone? In a tree? In an animal? In a heart encountered on the street? In a greeting or a kiss? Did we imagine only what we conventionally call scenes of beauty just now? Can we find God in a scene of political torture and murder or any of the countless other dark happenings? Jesus put it that we must sell all that we have to attain the pearl of great price, which is the sovereignty of God in our lives. Thus, we can say that God is redeemed when we pay the price to act for highest values. This kind of living is not yet what we most see about us in humanity. But where it happens, it does so because the ego is moved by the Self, or the God within, to take that step. I would describe this being moved also as *God seeking us*. We feel that we seek God, but the paradoxical contrast-nature of the cosmos applies even in respect of our search.

To continue with the same paradox, in seeking us out, along with who knows how many different species in the cosmos, God is also seeking redemption for creation. When we act from God within, we are helping God to do just that. It is relatively easy for us to imagine the redemption of creation in action for social justice. We must not forget, however, that God's joy also is ours when we look into the eyes of love in another person and realize God's joy in self-recognition. For us that is much more difficult, for it means that we must face the fact that we participate in God, and God in us, at all times.

Then, too, there is the experience of a personal relationship with God alone, such as when we must stand alone for a moral principle. It is embodied in acts of integrity and sacrifice, in which one has a sense of the divine presence and thus understands that one is serving a higher value on an individual basis.

Acceptance

The real struggle for us is not finding redemption from our neurotic anxiety but finding acceptance in the universe. Let the heart see its acceptance, and the redemption from neurosis will follow. After all, anxiety about being a part of the totality of reality, brought about by societal and familial notions as to what is and what is not "acceptable," lies at the root of most neurosis. The idea that God accepts us only on certain conditions, as taught in many forms of Christianity, has misled many Christians in their search for acceptance.[5] However, I do believe that there is a condition for acceptance, which is simply that we must not "render God ineffective within us," as Hebrew Scriptures scholar Charlene McCarthy put it.[6] Rendering God ineffective is actually quite difficult to do, though we certainly put God to sleep within us a lot.

Von Franz says that redemption is restored functioning.[7] I have always loved the following scene, which is in the same vein, from Franz Werfel's *Star of the Unborn*:

> *I had lost my friend, but I was not alone in the world. A group of young men who had witnessed the disaster ran toward me and took me in their midst. . . . They didn't sympathize with me, they weren't horrified, they didn't make long speeches, but immediately began a round dance.*
>
> *"Pain," said one, "is interruption of movement."*
> *"Healing," responded another, "is resumption of movement."*
> *"Alley-oop, Seigneur," whispered a third right beside me.*
> *"Relax, let go, lean."*[8]

Restored functioning is indeed healing, but in order for it to be redemption as well, the full subjective experience must be felt as of the utmost meaning or significance. Redemption involves a sense of being received by God: an internal "fitting in."

Seeing and Openness

The Godding is not just the operation of the Divine through individuals. Beyond this, there is a gradual building of the web of the universe in the form of interaction and communication of beings everywhere, so that the individual sparks of God can be experienced in ever wider, more comprehensive ways. We need eyes that can see in distance and depth. We need hearts that can feel in the same manner.

The world most needs the healing of the heart rather than the mind. True seeing is of the heart, as distinct from what we usually call seeing. The mind gives form to what the heart sees, what it is open to see, but we must become conscious of the fact that it is the heart that sees. When a light comes on, its energy floods the room. When we have an "aha" experience, we also feel a surge of energy. Seeing is the impact of energy: it is a heart thing. It is like the pumping of blood that carries energy to every part of our being.

However, interpretation attaches to us in every act of our seeing, physically or psychically, even in the case of seeing something as certain as the indubitable roundness of the earth. In a complete view that included the reality of field-knowledge and the fact that the inner/outer distinction is relative, even the common statement that the world is round would feel different from the same statement said in the present rationalistic world. *Even our hearts look out of us using the eyes of our times.*

If the only contrast-consciousness to which God has access is our ego-consciousness, then God also sees with the eyes of our times and thus knows (in a contrast manner) no more than we can guess. Sometimes we muse about what Moses or Buddha or Confucius or Jesus would make of the world if he could see it now. When we try to feel into what these religious leaders might feel, we are really attempting to feel what God might feel, because our God-image has been projected onto them. It is, then, a wonderful exercise to do this experiment. All scripture is human; it consists of humans feeling into what God might feel, even if words come with the objective force that we call inspiration. It is a deep way of looking with the heart. In the process, our assumptions about how the great religious figures would react ought to be taken as God's reaction. That has to be good enough for God at our present level of consciousness.[9]

Aliveness is feeling energy emerging, the patterned flow of energy from the depths of being, which Hindus call the "streams of *rta,"* *rta* being the Sanskrit term for the World-Order.[10] That is, the energy has a real though unrepresentable form: the Patterning. We tend to see only surface aspects of things. The task of re-envisioning is to look at the same thing again and see more deeply, by seeing the mystery that shines through everyday phenomena. For instance, the statement that the world is round may someday look incredibly simplistic, not because we will "know" that the world is indeed round but because the whole being of the world will have been reinterpreted in such a way that we will see newer depths in both what we know about the earth (and all things) and how we know it. That is, what we had thought of as a "clear understanding" as to the roundness of the world, based on measurement, will then be seen as an altogether infantile way of looking at reality. We will in fact employ more and more of our God-being in understanding reality, and it will enable us to see the God-being of things in the world.

Pain

Socrates said that true philosophers make dying their profession. This necessary dying is the dying of the ego-will, of boundaries and projections. It is most certainly painful to us in our egocentricity. But does God also suffer? I believe that the answer is yes, not just because of what we do to each other but because of our blindness. (Perhaps there is no difference between the two.) Does our unconsciousness cause suffering? Yes, emphatically and inevitably. But does it cause suffering for God? Under the Godding, insofar as it causes suffering to one of us, it causes it to the Self and to the divine being. But it is only conscious to the degree to which we both feel and know it. The same goes for avoidable partiality or fragmentedness, though no matter how conscious we become there will always be some partialness of being. This is due to the fact that we cannot ever become fully conscious, for that would be to exhaust the entire potential of the cosmos for creative being.

If we imagine God feeling joy at being seen, must we not also imagine the corresponding pain at remaining unseen? Then the universe was born in pain, billions of years before there was the least possibility for there to be a creature with an awareness of God. Is there a reality that corresponds to this imagining? The model of projection and recollection gives us one. If we imagine God suffering in some external form and realize that this is projection, then we know the suffering of God within.

The Anthropos *and Awakening*

There is a piece of God in each of us, which is precisely what unifies us, both as ourselves and with others. I said above that, when it breaks into concrete reality, the field remains unbroken, the God-image remains whole. In the case of humanity, the God-image ranges over the full spectrum of life and the symbols of nature, but it culminates in the image of the greater-than-human human, that is, in a human figure with divine attributes, referred to by early Gnostics and other Hellenistic groups as the *Anthropos*. (It has been difficult for Western cultures to render this figure in gender-neutral form; some Native Americans refer to it as "our grandfather the ancient woman." I like this very much, but I still like to use a single term where possible. The best candidate I know is *Anthropos*.)

I would like to picture the present era, say, the last two thousand years, as a time in which our awareness of the *Anthropos*, the Self, the Christ-within, or whatever you want to name the divine intermediary, is in a state of not quite being felt and realized by people in general.

Perhaps only when the seeing of a deep truth comes close to us or when we get close to the possibility of a new realization does a certain pain begin to grow, as when we are traveling and the road grade steepens. The question of speed and braking of a vehicle becomes relevant, and a kind of anxiety ensues. There is something shaking us, waking us up. The human waking to the reality of an inner Christ is also felt as shaking to us, as something impossible or dangerous. The road grade feels steep, and we hit the brakes.

But if we have been asleep, or if we have been keeping God asleep within, then it is better to wake. Our being asleep is a source of pain, at the least for the loss of the love in which we could have participated.

Let us then assume that a waking is imminent. A psychic sleep is the persistence of an undifferentiated whole, so that waking brings a new complexity. In our unconsciousness, we have assumed that we were in control, that the ego and its will were all there is to us. But now, as we look at ourselves, perhaps we feel something stirring, a realization of the fact that we are not alone within. Besides our ego with its contrast-knowledge, there are other kinds of knowing that we use, but we likely never thought much about how this other side of ourselves works and what the relation of the ego to it is.

I have called the "other" within ourselves various names as I have tried to illuminate our inner world somewhat: the prime inhabitant, the Self, the Christ within, the God within, or the God-image within, and now the *Anthropos*.

Let me address both myself and the reader in the following. Has the *Anthropos* suffered in you? Do you *know* the pain of having participated in the cause and protraction of this suffering, by delaying the waking? How do you *feel* about the *Anthropos*, this "anointed one," in you undergoing all this? It is a loss for God not to be awakened, but it is also your loss not to awaken to the God within. Is this not the most personal form of the suffering and death "for us and for our sake," as the Nicene Creed puts it? The end of this suffering is freedom—for only a consciousness that embodies that freedom is consciousness that fulfills the need of God in the human. Do you feel this for you? That is the requirement for it to be effective. Therefore the *Anthropos* must wait until the human consciousness "gets it" on its own; for, if it is gained in any other way, say, in blind adherence to a rote learning of a catechism, it is not attained through the individual's freedom. In psychological work with a helper, too, the guide cannot impart the needed insight as if it were a school fact to be learned but must lead one toward situations in which the insight may be encountered in freedom. In his foreword to the *I Ching,* Jung says: "Like a part of nature it waits until it is discovered."[11] Each of us must learn anew even the most important things that we learn as humans. "The burned hand teaches best."

The song asks, "Were you there?" at the crucifixion. That is exactly where we are—always—to the degree that we are conscious. Only under the criterion of consciousness do the opposites crucify. We do our best to remain unconscious in order to avoid this fact, to avoid pain, and in doing so, avoid joy and love as well. I have tried to stress that, when we face the darknesses and bring love, there is tremendous fulfillment. And only if we "take up our own cross" in consciousness do we alleviate the suffering of God. Until we embody this fact, our lives are instead a crucifixion of God. The cross is not only pain; it is the opposites, including the bright with the dark. It is the fullness of living that we fear to trust.

As we learn more and more to hold opposites together continuously without swinging like a pendulum from one contrast to another (as we do, say, between the conflicting needs of mercy and justice), we will begin to see beyond rational clarity and learn to include all of those ultimate facts of love that a rational understanding leaves out.

Theologian Martin Luther introduced the idea of the

priesthood of the believer. It is true that believers do form a priesthood, and infinitely more! We are responsible for the life of God-in-us.

What the Godding Does for God

To quote again from *Answer to Job:* "The human must, in order to survive, always be mindful of impotence. God has no need of this circumspection."[12] Jung is suggesting that for God there are no obstacles. I would add that God is immortal and need not consider either survival or death. By being immortal, God need not develop! But God does get frustrated and angry, because of what Jung calls "the unforeseen antics of [God's] creatures," and so *does* develop. Of course, we only say this because we experience something that we perceive or project as God's anger, but this is real under the hypothesis of Godding, and we will proceed in that light. Because God does not fear death, there is divine anger because we take it seriously, because we value our puny lives. But God needs this also, and we do well on all counts to value our lives and give this value to God.

Consciousness and death are thus seen to be most intimately bound together. The consciousness that God lacks is contrast-consciousness, which belongs to finitude. God needs our finitude. It is primarily this linkage of consciousness and death, to which God remains blind, that enters into our feelings and calculations and makes our "antics" unpredictable to God. We don't want to die. Curiously enough, our attitude reflects, in part, an attitude of God, though God cannot die! As Jung said, "God wants to become human, *but not quite,*" for that would be to encounter death.[13] However, if we live from the God-center, we also live by choosing the freedom that is offered in the present.

How does the anger of the ego at being in such a universe figure in the process? The ego has to learn the hard way that life is living, that there is a price for every gain. The price of holding the opposites is a "crucifixion." In fact, crucifixion is the symbol *par excellence* of holding the opposites together. Holding the opposites together is always a defeat for the egocentric will. Where does "salvation" arise? The following statement of Jung's is relevant here:

> *Like the alchemical adept, if we experience our own Self, the "true anthropos," in our opus, then we encounter the analogy of the anthropos—Christ—in new and direct form, and we recognize in the transformation in which we ourselves are involved a similarity to the Passion. It is not an "imitation of Christ" but its exact opposite: an assimilation of the Christ-image to our own Self, which is the "true anthropos.". . . The Passion happens to the adept, not in its classic form . . . but in the form expressed by the alchemical myth. It is the arcane substance that suffers those physical and moral tortures. . . . It is not the adept who suffers all this, rather it suffers in the adept, it is tortured, it passes through death and rises again. All this happens, not to the adept but to the "true anthropos," who the alchemist feels is not only near, but also within, and at the same time in the retort.*[14]

The goal of the "alchemical work," as of modern work at the transformative journey of the psyche, is just that of becoming a "new being." Through all that has been said here in demonstration that there is indeed a rebirth from our paradoxical sacrifice, I have tried to emphasize that we can experience the depth of joy and of love. If love does solve some of the problems of living, then our lives are indeed rewarded with something akin to the experience of Jesus at his baptism: the voice of God saying, "Thou art my beloved offspring, in whom I am well pleased."

CHAPTER 6

Fostering (Cosmic Ecology)

*If the doors of perception were cleansed
every thing would appear as it is, Infinite.*

For every thing that lives is Holy.

—WILLIAM BLAKE, *The Marriage of Heaven and Hell*

In chapter 3, we encountered two renowned scientists, one of whom found the cosmos "overwhelmingly hostile" and the other of whom found it to be "unexpectedly hospitable." Both of these feeling qualities would amount to what we have called projections onto the external cosmos, but at least they are ways of seeing the cosmos with the heart, for they engage the emotions. In this chapter, we will look at some facts that may help us to decide just how fostering of life the cosmos is.

At the same time, we will continue to look at the question of whether we are seeing the cosmos's own properties or projecting ours. We have seen some evidence that thinking of outer and inner as completely distinct is at least partially wrong. Is there really any difference in saying that the cosmos gives rise to beings who think and love or that it is itself loving in its own depth of being?

The fact that we have attributed love to an external God has been a way to keep spirit and matter separate. If we are coming to see the physical cosmos as the body of God, we can bring love into physical reality, seeing it as an attribute of spirit-matter, by reason of the freedom that is one of its inherent characteristics.

This is the second of three chapters that bring to the book the scientific view of the cosmos. Its role in our exploration is to show how fully the ecology of the cosmos favors life. We can then use our own feelings to judge its hospitality, or caring, and to see it as a heart-cosmos. Thus it is an essential section of the book, allowing us to exercise our ability to respond to this view of the cosmos with our hearts.

Big Stars, Small Stars

Whether or not it is intentional on the part of a supreme power, the "system" of the cosmos does serve the evolution of life. The evidence for this remarkable fact can be found by examining three fundamental things:

1. The underlying principles of physical reality, which we explored in chapter 1 and the beginning of chapter 2[1]
2. The specific quantitative relations of physical forces and "particles," which were given brief mention in chapter 4, item 2[2]
3. The outcome of the first two in processes that occur on a cosmic scale.

It is this third item that we will examine now, in order to see how life evolves in the cosmos.

Stars come in a tremendous range of sizes. Actually, the planet Jupiter is an "almost star," at about one thousandth of the mass of the sun. The largest stable stars are about fifty times the massiveness of the sun. At roughly one-and-a-third solar masses, a division can be made between small stars and big ones, for the general behavior of stars in the two groups is quite different with respect to the questions we are asking.

Stars that have planets will generally be small; big stars probably will not have planets. Small stars live long lives, while big ones are short-lived. By "long," I mean long enough for life to evolve to consciousness. Small stars do not explode, while big ones do. To me this is quite remarkable. If a certain kind of star typically formed planets, but either did not live long enough for life to evolve on those planets or did live long enough but was likely to prove a destroying inferno in a cataclysmic blast, we would consider the cosmos much less hospitable to life, for life emerges and grows to consciousness on the planets.

But that is only the start. In general, since planetary systems follow a model similar to our own solar system (for reasons that will be given), then it is likely that an earthlike, or "terrestrial," planet will follow an orbit at about the right distance from its "parent" star. The energy received from the parent star needs to be such that the planet is neither too hot nor too cold, which is defined by the range between the freezing point of water and about a third of the way from the freezing to the boiling point. This is called the "life zone" around the parent sun. The model that will be outlined for the formation of solar systems also predicts that, as planets form, their matter is "coated" with the molecules of which living organisms are made. They are "primed" for life.

It is also the case that none of this wonderful scenario would be possible if it were not for the big stars. Because they live short lives and then explode, the stars that are not going to form planetary systems contribute the materials out of which planets are made: the elements heavier than helium.

These big stars start out with about three-fourths of their mass in the form of hydrogen, the lightest element, and one-fourth as helium, the next lightest. During the lives of these stars, the hydrogen and helium are converted to heavier elements in nuclear fusion processes. This nuclear "burning" releases the energy that we see as starshine. Hydrogen and helium are the "fuel" and the heavier elements are the "ash." When stars run out of fuel, they are unable to maintain the pressure in their cores, which is normally supplied by the release of energy in nuclear burning. They then collapse, but this collapse initiates an explosion of all the unburned material in the outer parts of the star, and through this process the unburned material is converted to heavier elements. This explosion is as bright as the light of all the hundreds of billions of stars in a galaxy put together. In a typical galaxy, such "supernovas" occur every century or so, and if they occur in our own galaxy, they may be bright enough for us to see even in daytime. The heavy elements that are produced in this burst, amounting to about half the mass of the original big star, are then blown away and scattered through space, mixing with primordial hydrogen and helium in gas clouds that have not yet begun the process of becoming stars.

When these enriched clouds of hydrogen and helium do form into stars, they then possess the needed heavier elements out of which to make planets. Our own sun formed from such an enriched cloud. The heavier elements out of which our planet, and we ourselves, are made, were produced in one or more supernova explosions that enriched our region of the Milky Way galaxy. We are, literally, stardust. Figure 6.1 gives a brief summary:

	SMALL STARS	BIG STARS
Does it have planets?	Yes	No
What is its lifetime?	Long	Short
Does it explode?	No	Yes
What is the consequence?	Terrestrial planets in the life zone, with life molecules	Recycling and enriching of stellar material; creation of new cosmoi

FIGURE 6.1 *How small and big stars contribute to the evolution of life in the cosmos*

How Planets Are Formed

Our sun is spinning at about one revolution every three-and-a-half weeks. Most small stars spin at similar rates. Big stars spin about a hundred times faster, on average. The story of how planets are formed is intimately related to this difference in spin. The origin of starspin, and the reason there is such uniformity of spin, lies in the rotation of the entire Milky Way Galaxy, which makes one complete rotation about every two hundred and fifty million years. It is slow and majestic, having made about forty full turns since it was first formed about ten billion years ago.

Every cloud of gas and dust that is about to form into a star rotates with the galaxy. These clouds are very large and tenuous. In order to contain enough material to form a star like our sun, such a cloud must be several light-years in diameter or about twenty trillion miles.

Light from the sun reaches Earth in about eight minutes, at "light speed."[3] It takes light over four years to cover the distance from the Sun to the nearest star, Alpha Centauri. On a scale where Earth was one foot from the sun, Alpha Centauri would be about as far away as the distance from San Francisco to Chicago.

Let us return to the rotating gas cloud. In forming a star, it shrinks under the mutual gravitational attraction of its own material. This takes a long time, which is partly why, even after the ten billion years our galaxy has lived, some such clouds are still in the process of forming stars. Some do it in much less time, but a billion years is still typical. As spinning things contract, they spin faster, like the spinning ice-skater who pulls in his or her arms and leg to achieve the rapid rotation that we see. Just as the skater's rotation falls into a predictable range of rapidity because of the typical conditions under which it is begun, so also the clouds that form stars should fall into a predictable range. In fact, the spin of the larger stars confirms the prediction. Starspin arises from original spin of the galaxy.

If the small stars have thus lost most of their spin, where did it go? Like energy, spin is a conserved quantity. If you could tie a cable to each of the planets in the solar system and haul them in to the Sun, in the manner that the skater pulls in arms and leg, the Sun would spin at just the right rate to fit into the prediction from original galactic spin. The conclusion is that the missing spin went into the formation of the planets. Since most small stars spin slowly, a good first guess is that they mostly form planets.

This guess does indeed account for half of the small stars. With the rest, the shrinking cloud breaks up and forms two stars in tight orbits around each other. These are called binary systems. It turns out that binary systems are easily detected by analyzing their light. So we know that about half of small stars are binaries, and we conclude that the other half probably form planetary systems. Of the four hundred billion stars in the Milky Way galaxy, we can be conservative by taking only half of what we expect to be there, so we guess that about one hundred billion must have planetary systems.

If one in a thousand of these had a terrestrial planet in the life zone, we would then have a hundred million planets about as well located to evolve life as is our own Earth. Astronomer Fred Hoyle has outlined a highly probable scenario for the transfer of spin from the sun to the forming planets.[4]

As a protostar shrinks, it spins faster and faster, as noted earlier. The centrifugal force is greatest at its equator, and as the spin increases, at a certain point the centrifugal force becomes as strong as the attraction of gravity. The star then begins to leave the material at the equator behind as it shrinks. This is referred to as "spinning a disk." (See figure 6.2.) The diagram shows a cross-section of the shrinking star and the development of the disk.

Notice that the disk does not fly away or expand away from the star. Not yet:

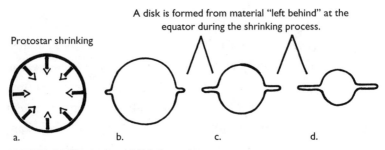

FIGURE 6.2 *The process of disk formation*

The protostar is also heating up, because the very shrinkage releases energy. In chapter 1, I referred to this principle of the release of energy as "the prime law of physics," because all energy in the cosmos has its source in the fact that, if material moves closer together under an attracting force, or moves further apart under a repelling force, energy is released. This law is obeyed by all of the four forces of physics, from nuclear to gravitational. Gravity is the weakest of the four by far, but it has a special quality that permits it to dominate the major events in the cosmos. While the other forces exhibit both attraction and repulsion, gravity only attracts. The other forces average themselves out to zero on the large scale of astronomical phenomena. Since gravity only pulls and does not push, nothing can shield matter from attraction by all other matter in the cosmos. In the cosmos as a whole and even for single stars, therefore, gravity dominates.

As the protostar shrinks, it also becomes more opaque, like a thickening haze, and the energy that is generated within it escapes only with more and more difficulty.

About the time that the star is spinning a disk, it has become so hot in its core that its nuclear processes are turned on.

One more fact. We observe that the sun and all other stars

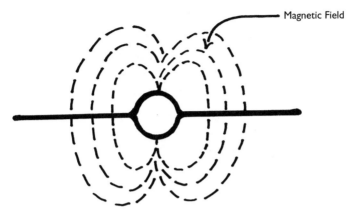

FIGURE 6.3 Expansion of disk due to increased spin from magnetic field

have *magnetic fields*. Just as in the case of spin, this uniformity derives from a quality of the galaxy as a whole, in this case its magnetic field. A magnetic field can be "trapped" in very hot gases because the gases exert a drag on the field. This is not like picking up bits of iron with an iron magnet. It is more like dragging a fishing net through the ocean. The protostar is spinning faster than the disk, and its magnetic field is trying to pass through the spun-off disk, but the disk, consisting of very hot gases, causes a drag on the field. The drag tends to slow down the star and to speed up the rotation of the disk, so that the spin of the star is decreased while that of the disk is increased. This amounts to a transfer of the spin from the star to the disk.

As the disk takes up the spin from the protostar, it is accelerated in its orbit, which causes it to expand, that is, to move away from the star. As it gets more distant from the main source of heat, it cools. (See figure 6.3.)

As it cools, material begins to condense out of the hot cloud, beginning with those with the highest boiling points. The materials that have the highest boiling points, and also happen to be most abundant in the cloud, are iron and the constituents of rock, largely silicon dioxide. These condensations should be in the form of droplets, which become pellets when they pass below their melting temperatures. These bits of matter no longer drag on the magnetic field of the rotating star, and so are left behind, resulting in a wide band of pellets of rock and iron. Later, when the expanding disk is much more distant from the star, the other main abundances will condense out. These are gases: hydrogen, helium, and methane.

Here is the clincher. We find that the first four planets nearest the Sun, Mercury, Venus, Earth, and Mars, are planets that consist mostly of rock and iron. The next four major planets, Jupiter, Saturn, Uranus, and Neptune, are mainly gaseous planets, consisting of the gases just mentioned. Because of the fixed relationship between the heat of the star and the condensation of rock and iron, the likelihood becomes very great that a rock and iron (terrestrial) planet will be formed in the life zone of the star. My own guess suggests that maybe one in ten planetary systems has a planet favorably located for the evolution of life. I feel that the one-in-a-thousand estimate given above is quite conservative and that it is overwhelmingly likely that there are at least a hundred million planets in our Milky Way Galaxy alone, each of which is as favorably located with respect to its sun as Earth is with respect to our sun.

Interlude: Bent Space

It is a creative universe and an efficient one at that! With hundreds of billions of other galaxies, our cosmos is full of life beyond any reasonable doubt. However, there's more—much more. In order to see the really overwhelming potential for the abundance of life, we need to look at the so-called black holes, which are the apparent remains of massive stars that have blasted away about half of their material in supernova explosions.

A little speculation here may not be out of place, if I

emphasize that what has just been presented is not very speculative at all. We have yet to devote any significant energy to joining the intragalactic network of communication that almost without question must exist out there, but it has been wisely cautioned that we will not be likely do so until we have learned to function as a whole planet first.

The speculation, then. The whole nature of our cosmos is not assuredly known. The best thought at the moment is that the cosmos is either (1) self-contained, a space bent around itself by its own gravitational pull; or (2) not bent, but "flat," so that it extends outward infinitely. My own leanings are to the first option.

Here is a model for visualizing a "bent" space in two dimensions, using the third of our spatial dimensions to see the bending of the two. A two-dimensional space is like an infinitely thin piece of paper or like one of our ordinary maps. On a map, we need only two numbers to locate a point, namely, longitude and latitude. Now let us visualize a *rubber* map and pull the corners together, so that we can make it into a balloon and blow it up. We still need only two numbers, longitude and latitude, to locate any point on the map, but now it is curved around itself. If we now picture the map as a balloon with the map painted on it, without the "navel" that a balloon has, but we could still arrange to blow it up so that it can be expanded, we are ready to proceed. Now we could picture a tiny being, who can move around *in the rubber* of the balloon. Every point to which the being can go can be specified using only a longitude and a latitude. Therefore, it is still a two-dimensional space, though we see it curved around itself in three dimensions. Life for us on the surface of Earth is somewhat like that of the being, for the Earth's surface is curved, though we do not ordinarily notice it. We have to get to a high vantage point to do so. We suppose it is the same for the tiny being. Though we have a vantage point in the third dimension, the being does not notice the curvature.

The being has at its disposal only two basic ways to move:

left/right and forward/backward. These are the two dimensions. It cannot even conceive of up/down, for that would take it out of the rubber, which is its "space." Thus it can travel anywhere within its space without discovering a boundary. The space is "unbounded." We (as three-dimensional beings looking on from outside) can see, however, that the space is not unlimited in extent; that it simply curves around and rejoins itself, so that the being might be going around and around the ball and think it was going on forever.

Let us try to transfer this metaphor to our own real space-time system. If our own cosmos is closed, from our point of view it shares these two qualities of being finite, but unbounded. At any moment, it has a definite volume (as the balloon had a definite surface area) but no boundaries. If we travel through our space in a spaceship, we can execute commands to turn in directions such as left/right, forward/backward, and up/down, but we cannot even conceive of a direction "out." We are helped a bit by our fourth dimension, time, and the fact that space is expanding, to see that the "center" of our space is the point of origination in the Big Bang, fifteen billion years ago. The "center" is not in our space now.[5]

Our cosmos is definitely expanding. Those who think that the cosmos is bent or closed believe that there is not enough energy in the motion of expansion for the matter to break clear of the gravitational forces that bend it back on itself. Those who feel that it is "flat" feel that it has just enough energy that it will take an infinite time for matter to coast to a halt against the pull of its own gravity. The observations that would settle the matter for all concerned have to do with finding all the forms of matter in the cosmos and totaling them up to see whether there is just enough to make it "flat" or whether there is more, which would mean that there is enough to pull the expanding cosmos to a stop in a finite time, after which it will collapse again and perhaps bounce again into expansion after that.

I feel, though, that there is another way of looking at it. If energy is the source of the cosmos, then there should be both positive and negative forms of energy, so that the total energy of the cosmos is zero. As far as I know, this idea was first published by physicist Marcel Golay in 1961.[6] There are three forms of positive energy: the energy-content of matter itself, the energy of motion of matter, and radiant energy in the form of light and other electromagnetic waves. There is just one form of negative energy, namely, the gravitational relationship of the matter and energy in the cosmos.

The argument is that if not all of the positive energy is in the motion of matter, then the motion of matter cannot be so great as to overcome the gravitational relationship of the whole, since the negative energy of gravitational relationship is enough to balance all three positive forms. This is why other physicists and I feel that enough matter will be found to account for the closing, in spite of the popularity of "inflationary" cosmology, which predicts that the cosmos is flat.

Black Holes and Abundance

When a big star explodes as a supernova, about half of its original stuff is left over as a tiny, rapidly spinning "neutron star." A neutron star is so dense that each cubic centimeter contains a hundred million tons of neutrons. To visualize a hundred million tons, imagine plucking up a good-sized mountain or a middling city and squeezing it all into one cubic centimeter.

If the total amount of matter that comprises the neutron star is greater than about one-and-a-third solar masses, then the gravity of the neutron star will be strong enough to crush that star out of existence, by squeezing it to such an extent that its own gravity will be so strong that light cannot escape it. Since light is the measure of space (light rays define straight lines), this means that gravity has bent the star's space around it, as we bent the map into a balloon to give the model of the closed two-dimensional cosmos earlier. A space bent completely around itself so that light cannot escape is known as a "black hole." In his 1961 paper, Golay suggested that we could create a cosmos if we could make a black hole, but he did not go so far as to say that stars that enter the black hole state do so. The name and the connection with neutron stars did not then exist. But now we can make the connection. The configuration of both the cosmos and the interior of a black hole is the same. Each is a three-dimensional closed space. We may be inside what is a simple black hole in another cosmos. The shrinking of a neutron star in that other cosmos may have given birth to this cosmos of ours.

There is one apparent difficulty: the black hole formed by the death of a star is very small compared to a cosmos. However, this difficulty is only apparent. If we can create gravitational relationship, that is, create negative energy, we also create positive energy, with a net cost of zero. After all, this is what our present cosmos is now: something whose total energy content is zero. In going into the black hole state, a star is generating more and more of both positive and negative energy. The positive energy can be ascribed to the prime law of physics mentioned above, and the negative energy can be ascribed to the fact that the matter in the black hole is getting closer and closer together. There is no theoretical limit as to how much energy can be created in this manner. To produce a whole cosmos as massive as our own is not out of the question. In Golay's original paper, he suggested making a cosmos by making a black hole of much smaller size than a neutron star.

Thus, the note in the table (figure 6.1) at the start of this section: big stars make new *cosmoi* (the plural of cosmos), and the abundance of this potential for new life absolutely overwhelms the mere hundred million living planets in a galaxy.

Re-envisioning Spinoff

How does all this help us to re-envision the cosmos with the heart? Let us begin where we left off, with the sense of a tremendous abundance. In each cosmos are hundreds of billions of galaxies, each, on the average, with millions of life-bearing planets evolving toward greater consciousness and deeper spirituality. Secondly, we also sense *caring*, in that life, once begun in some place in a cosmos, will have the duration available for the evolution of a significant consciousness, because stars that foster planets last a long time and do not explode.

Thirdly, we can sense a gentleness in the cosmos, in that it provides for life on the planets, rather than in the atmospheres of the stars. As violent as conditions on Earth can be with storms and earthquakes and such, a planet is a much more gentle place than a star. I will explain.

We can link the strength of the forces of the universe to the "repertoire" of what can be done with spirit-matter. Nuclear forces are the strongest, and several hundred nuclear species exist. The bonds between atoms in inorganic chemistry are much more gentle, and hundreds of thousands of inorganic compounds exist. The bonds of organic and life chemistry are more gentle still, and their repertoire is unlimited. The more gentle the bonds between things, the greater the repertoire, or the variety of combinations, that can be made with those things.

We can carry the same inverse relationship on into consciousness and love, so that the possibilities of gentle things vastly outnumber those of relationships based on strength.

For instance, we see this inverse variation in the relationship of human violence to consciousness, which generally preclude each other. Another is that the stronger stuff of jealousy stands in the way of love, whose goal is that the loved one be free. The more subtle the bonds (in terms of physical energy and even psychic energy), the more varied and interesting life can be.

This theme can be woven through all that we have done. The individual must shake loose many chains in order to live in freedom but can then establish a living relationship with others in the world. These chains, which William Blake called "the mind-forged manacles," include some of our cultural and religious mindsets. The individual also must shake loose the bonds of egocentricity in order to find the subtle Self who has been waiting in each of us for this freeing to work itself through. This is no less than the message of the whole structure of the cosmos, as it is becoming known.

Science itself has been an attempt to employ psychic strength, in the form of logical necessity, to the vision of the cosmos. Even those of us without a rigorous scientific training can see how hard it is to give up the idea that the intellect should be dominant in the scientific enterprise. But as life in the universe becomes more complex, we begin to see the need to engage the heart in understanding the cosmos, if only for our survival. If we got no further than re-envisioning science with the heart, we would take a major step toward ensuring the continuance of life on Earth.

From what we have seen of the tuning of the cosmos for the support of life, it is clear that we would then be aligning our hearts with the evident intent of the universe.

CHAPTER 7

Physical Gathering and Layering

*In the beginning, in the small and the great darkness,
life is not Something; it ardently Is. Beginnings
are not precision. Beginnings are not confusion.
They are darkness drawn to a minute point of nondarkness, and silence gathered into a small sound.*

—SHEILA MOON, *A Magic Dwells*

It seems to be about time for taking stock of what we have made of our enterprise of re-envisioning the cosmos with the heart up to the present point. It is not only that we are including heart-qualities in the cosmos as we look at it from a distance. Science might say, "All right, we see that we must include life in our view of the evolution of the physical universe, but don't ask us to get involved with it, and please don't wave God and spirituality at us. It is necessary that we hold out for the most rational world possible." But if we see the cosmos with the heart, that is, from our deeper being, if we open ourselves to the cosmos in that way, then we do indeed involve ourselves in the mutual support of life, and we also must abandon any limits as to how far we are willing to go with our openness.

If spirit and matter are simply the two faces of the stuff of the universe, if we are free by the very nature of spirit-matter, and if interaction leads to wounding but also the possibility of healing, because the cosmos sets problems that only love can solve, then seeing the cosmos with the heart means precisely going all the way with it, just as seeing any human being with the heart confronts us with the same demand.

Once we have the possibility of the Godding, the whole path is indeed in view, but there still is much that can be brought out to clarify the picture. And perhaps the locks of our hearts need the application of more rust penetrants. I feel that, as we see and understand more, we can accept more and that *facts* are gentle hammers with which to work on the psyche.

The heart vision includes the mind vision. I have been using the scientific images of the cosmos and of microphysical entities such as electrons and photons in such a way that, as components of the more partial scientific view, they serve the more inclusive and deeper vision of the heart. I will take the same perspective in this chapter. The story of gathering and layering in the cosmos serves to illustrate the more universal process of evolution in the Godding cosmos.

I will begin with a brief summary of the parallels between physical processes (to be treated in this chapter) and psychic processes (to be treated in chapter 8).

Gathering

In the first chapter, I discussed how the source of all energy in the cosmos is the gathering of material under the influence of an attracting force. Because of this universality, I called this law of energy release the "prime law" of physics. This is my own name for

PHYSICAL GATHERING AND LAYERING

this overarching process; it will not be found in a physics book. The only source that does not obviously follow this pattern is the burst of energy that was the Big Bang itself, unless it can be seen as a contraction or gathering of God.

The epigraph that begins this chapter came in a dream to my friend and teacher Sheila Moon. It expresses the idea of the prime law in terms both mythic and psychological. The fact that this beautiful expression of inner reality is also good physics speaks of the ultimate sense of gathering in this book. There is a common structure that unifies spirit and matter in what Teilhard called spirit-matter.

In chapter 5, I described the process whereby a living being comes to greater consciousness as a parallel to the cosmic process of evolution of the patterned stuff of the universe following the Big Bang. Then, using the image of the cosmic pawn shop, I spoke of the gathering of God and the whole cosmos into one's being. Consciousness, leading toward God's self-consciousness, is the apparent goal of the creation and evolution of the cosmos, for it is the leading phenomenon presently unfolding the evolutionary possibilities of spirit-matter.

In this chapter and the next, we continue to fill in the parallels in the process of gathering and the formation of layers, using the life story of a star (which was begun in chapter 6) as the model. The parallels lie between the arising and evolution of galaxies and stars in the cosmos on the one hand and the arising and evolution of consciousness in human societies and individuals on the other. The parallelism will be highlighted by depicting both with the same set of diagrams. In each case, we can ask these questions: what is gathered; by what is the gathering done; and what is the result of the gathering?

The symbolic answer to the first question—what is gathered?—is some sort of elementary bits of stuff that are physical in the case of the stars and psychic in the case of consciousness. In the case of the physical cosmos, it is the atoms, formed from the material created in the Big Bang, which are gathered. In the case of the psyche, it is "psychic contents" or pattern-fragments. When we have an "aha!" experience, something is gathered to the part of our psyche accessible to the ego and becomes part of the structure of our consciousness.

In the physical cosmos, that which gathers is what we call gravity. There is also a mutual attractiveness of the elements of the psyche, which might be called a sort of psychic gravity.

What is formed is something that can contain the energy generated through the gathering process itself. Physically, this is the star and the galaxy that contains the star. Psychically, the container that is formed is the ego and the Self that contains the ego. This is just a bare outline, of course. The parallelism of the two processes suggests a unity of structure in the whole of reality.[1]

Beginnings

When the cosmos emerged as a burst of intense energy in the Big Bang, its energy content was many billions of times greater than its matter content.[2] In this primordial energy "soup," matter, in the form of quarks and leptons, was flowing continually out of the energy and being reabsorbed into it (like croutons and pieces of chicken in an ordinary soup suddenly appearing to view and then disappearing, while all the time the total amount of croutons and chicken in the soup remain constant). Quarks are the particles that combine to form the more familiar protons and neutrons that comprise the atomic nucleus, while the most familiar "lepton" is the ordinary electron.[3]

The cosmos was unimaginably hot and dense, containing, in a volume smaller than the nucleus of one of our atoms, far more "stuff" than now remains in our entire visible universe, that is, not only the billions of galaxies seen with astronomical instruments but immense amounts of "dark matter" besides. It was a seething,

PHYSICAL GATHERING AND LAYERING

patterned energy field, giving birth to and reabsorbing various types of quark-pairs and lepton-pairs. The creation of pairs of particles is stressed because the two members of a pair have opposed properties that can cancel out again if similarly opposed particles meet. If all the properties cancel, then the two particles disappear and return to a pure energy form.

By the patterning of the field, I do not mean something that can be visualized geometrically, but instead I am suggesting that there was a limit on the kinds of particles that could be produced by the energy soup, and their properties are something today's physicists think they know. It could not and did not produce an infinite variety.

As it expanded and cooled, it may be that conditions occurred that caused it to "inflate" for a brief time, continuing to fill with the energy-quark-lepton mix until it had multiplied itself many billion-fold. It is likely to be a long time before we have an adequate grasp of these earliest cosmic conditions. At some point, the expanding cosmos cooled to the point that it no longer kept producing quarks and leptons, and the remaining quarks then combined to form protons. As the cosmos cooled still further (being then nearly two minutes old!), some of the protons combined with each other to form helium nuclei, as I described in the first chapter, but the cosmos was still too hot for the protons and helium nuclei to come together with electrons to form atoms of hydrogen and helium. For that, it had to expand for three hundred thousand more years. If we let that time pass in our minds, we have set the stage for the images of gathering.

Once it was cool enough, the protons and helium nuclei, with their positive electric charge, attracted the negatively charged electrons and combined with them into atoms that were electrically neutral. Since the newly neutral atoms were not gripped by the energy field in the way that the charged particles were, we say that the energy field was "uncoupled" from the atoms that were

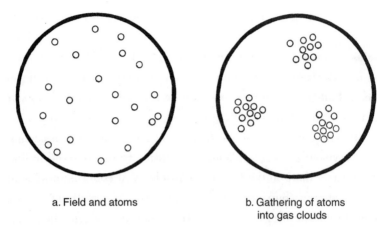

a. Field and atoms   b. Gathering of atoms into gas clouds

FIGURE 7.1. Gathering

then drifting throughout it. This left the atoms free to draw together by means of their mutual gravity. The "gathering" diagram is in figure 7.1.

Note that gravity both unites atoms with those nearby and separates the various gatherings of atoms from each other. Some atoms get closer while the clouds get farther apart. This is called the "fragmentation" of the original gas cloud. These first gatherings (gas clouds) became clusters and superclusters of galaxies. Each such cloud then fragmented further into smaller clouds that become galaxies, and each galaxy-cloud finally fragmented into stars. We thus have three layers of physical gathering so far, each of which can use the very same diagram: the cosmos gathering into major gas clouds, the major gas clouds gathering into galaxies, and galaxies gathering into stars.

In chapter 6, I presented the life of a protostar from its beginning as a cloud of gas and dust that starts out several light-years in size. Gradually, it gathers under the mutual gravitational attraction of its own internal parts, and in the process of shrinking, it concentrates its share of original galactic spin into its own rapid rotation. When it is rotating fast enough, it spins off a disk of material

PHYSICAL GATHERING AND LAYERING

and then transfers nearly all of its spin to the disk. As the protostar contracts, it also heats up and begins to shine, for the contraction releases energy under the "prime law." Thus, it literally fits the description of the epigraph: "darkness gathered into a minute point of nondarkness."

The interior of the protostar eventually becomes so hot that the processes of nuclear fusion begin to release their own energy, and the star begins to shine using energy from its own interior nuclear processes. The initial burst of energy from this new source stirs up the material of the star, with the result that it suddenly becomes very bright, heating the material of the disk even further, as it moves away from the protostar to the regions where the planets will be. Then the star "settles" into the condition it will maintain for billions of years, and the material of the disk cools and condenses into the pellets that will gather into the planets. Here I am speaking mostly of the earthlike rock and iron planets that can harbor the evolution of life as we know it.

Layering

From here, we go on to the layering that develops in a star as it goes through its normal lifetime. The layers form in a star as a consequence of the gathering, as will be seen.

The star is hottest at the center and relatively cool on the surface. For instance, the center of the Sun has a temperature of about fifty million degrees Fahrenheit, and a surface temperature of a mere ten thousand degrees. The nuclear fusion, or "nuclear burning," requires temperatures in the tens of millions of degrees, so that it only happens near the center. The region of nuclear burning is called the core. In this core, the hydrogen "fuel" gradually is converted to helium "ash."

To give a simple picture, let us say that this burning is steady until the fuel runs out. The burning supplies heat, which maintains the pressure in the star's interior. (This image works for the psyche, too: when we are "hot," there is a lot of internal "pressure.") The nuclear burning is so steady, and the available energy is so abundant, that the star's condition is stable for many billions of years: the pull of gravity tending to collapse the star is balanced by the pressure based on its internal heat.

When all of the hydrogen is used up in the core, there is no more hydrogen burning to produce heat. Thus, this source of pressure begins to fail, and the core begins to shrink. This shrinking, under the "prime law," releases more energy, and the core temperature rises, increasing the pressure again somewhat. But the gravity has become stronger, since some shrinking has occurred and the force of gravitational attraction is greater the closer together things are. With this stronger squeeze, the central temperature becomes greater than before.

At its new higher temperature, the center of the core is able to begin burning helium into carbon, nitrogen, and oxygen. The ash of the previous stage of burning becomes fuel for the next. Where this new form of burning is going on then becomes a new core. A new layer has been added at the center. The diagram of this stage of layering can be seen in figure 7.2a.

Moreover, the layer just outside the original core now becomes hot enough that the hydrogen there can begin conversion to helium. The result is that the layer in which hydrogen is burned to become helium moves gradually outward, and a new layer is added

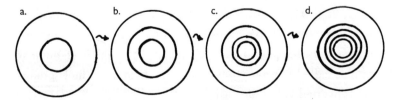

FIGURE 7.2 Layering: Each new layer is formed at the center, where things are hotter, and moves outward from there.

at the center of the star, in which the products of the previous burning stage become the fuel for the next. Our discussion has now reached the stage shown in figure 7.2b.

Since nuclear burning fuses the fuel particles, leaving a heavier ash particle, the areas of burning become continually more dense, so that gravity has a stronger and stronger grip on the core of the star, and ever higher temperatures are needed to prevent its collapse.

The adding of a new core at the center of the star continues through several stages, with more and more complex elements forming at the center and more and more layering of the star's interior.

When the complexity developed by fusing simpler elements together builds to the level of elements like iron, nickel, and cobalt, the burning has reached its limit. Iron is the ultimate nuclear ash. The only way to produce the full range of elements that we know, including those heavier than iron, such as mercury, lead, gold, and uranium, is by means of a supernova explosion. The process of building these heavier-than-iron elements absorbs energy rather than releasing it.

The energy of a supernova is supplied under the "prime law" by the sudden gravitational collapse of the innermost (iron) core of a star (such as the one pictured in figure 7.2d) when nuclear burning can no longer supply heat to maintain the pressure needed to prevent that collapse. Since presenting the picture of gathering and layering was the object of telling the star's story, we need not concern ourselves with either the mechanism of this collapse or the evolution of the outward appearance of the star through all these processes.

To review the whole cosmic process: about three hundred thousand years following the emergence of matter out of the original burst of energy in the Big Bang, the material particles that had been produced in the Big Bang began a series of gatherings. The first of these gathered the material of the first three minutes into great clouds that would become clusters of galaxies. These then subdivided (gathered) into galactic whorls containing the clouds that then further fragmented and gathered into smaller clouds that finally would gather into stars.

Since the cosmos was the outcome of a tremendous explosion, the matter was not uniform, but somewhat raggedly distributed, though other forces had been at work trying to make the whole more uniform, in the time before atoms could form. But if matter is a little more dense in some places, gravity can pull it together toward those places, away from the less dense places. This is how fragmentation and gathering occur together, as shown in figure 7.1, the gathering diagram. As the stars live out their lives, they undergo layering in the manner we have just seen.

Stars do not form all at once. As mentioned in chapter 6, about half of the smaller stars that form later, after some of the bigger stars have exploded and enriched the remaining gas clouds with heavy elements, form planets in the process of being born.

Gathering Life

In those planetary systems in which an earthlike planet happens to be at a favorable distance from its parent sun, the life molecules that coat the materials out of which the planets gathered begin themselves to gather in pools of water, sometimes called primordial planetary soup, as distinct from the cosmic soup described earlier in this chapter.

Again the "gathering" diagram applies, as seen in figure 7.3.

The dotted circles are added around the "organisms" to signify the containment that they possess. Something has been added to the cosmos: skin. A star is not held together by an external membrane but only by its internal gravity. And yet the gathering of

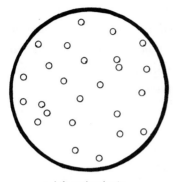
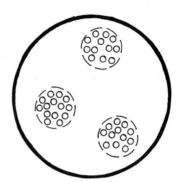

a. Life molecules in planetary soup.

b. Life molecules gathering into organisms.

FIGURE 7.3 *Gathering life*

more inert life molecules with an exterior protective and containing function is a form of layering, which gives a tremendous boost to the efficiency of whatever is going on inside.

The gathering thus also becomes the taking-in of nutrients from the soup. The most "effective" organism gets the greater share of the food. Life, in its simplest forms, has actualized itself.

I want to suggest that there is an analogy between the taking-in of nutrients and the retrieval of formerly projected psychic contents that results in the growth of the organism of the spirit. For example, if I have an overwhelmingly negative emotional reaction to members of a particular group, say motorcycle clubs ("gangs!") and then discover humanity among them, I am then both stronger and more open; less fearful. I am nourished. In this sense, too, the most effective organisms get the greater share of the food, but in psychic nutrition, the same food can nourish many, as can be seen in the case of art.

In the "primordial life-soup" that exists on the surface of an evolving earthlike planet, life can have no definite beginning. Everywhere are attractions, gatherings, bondings. Here, again, the idea of life as fundamental disequilibrium applies, and evolution simply proceeds because it must. The life-molecules themselves have been built up in the expanding disk of material moving away from the spinning sun (chapter 6), even before Earth was fully coagulated out of the disk. All of the building blocks of proteins and DNA, the amino acids and the nucleotides, were already present. They only needed a medium, water (the soup), for their gathering and bonding to occur.

Of the elements heavier than hydrogen and helium, carbon plays the major part in life chemistry. Other elements that are near it in weight, such as nitrogen and oxygen, are also much involved. With carbon as catalyst, and hydrogen also playing a part, these elements form the amino acids and nucleotides that make up our protein and DNA. As noted in chapter 1, molecules "contain" the beginnings of "the within of things"; and when they gather to build into elementary organisms in the soup, this inwardness also complexifies and becomes psyche, the "container" of the Self. The words *contain* and *container* are in quotes because there is a paradox in the analogy with regard to the psyche, namely, that the Self also contains the psyche and the whole "within of things." The paradox just named embodies the "archaic identity of subject and object," which will be discussed again below as it applies to humans: *the object contains the subject and the subject contains the object.*

In the long evolutionary process, the life-molecules of Earth gather and complexify into Earth's myriad subjects, the aware living beings in the local part of the cosmos, though the field is the field of the whole cosmos and is not just local. It not only bears the imprint of the whole from all the energy exchanges of the past, but the whole is always present at every point. Since the cosmos contains all physically, it becomes the ultimate spirit-matter object-of-contemplation for the subject. Let us now return to the process.

In the next evolutionary level of being, the new elements of life, single-cell organisms, gather through movement and interaction. As I am not a biologist, my description of the following stages will be somewhat sketchy. For over a billion years, the evolutionary development was mostly confined within a major form known as blue-green algae, which contains the roots of both plant and animal life. This next level is more complex, more flexible. In it, the within becomes capable of response to stimulus in a fashion that is characteristic of the organism. Responses became both more varied and more definite. This cosmic "cooking" worked toward self-reflexivity by building psyche, which I see as the inwardness aspect of things mentioned above.[4]

In the third general level, known in paleobiology as the "Cambrian Explosion," there was a vast differentiation of life-forms, a symbolic beginning of the whole movement of life toward individuation *within* species, which in our own time is at last becoming manifest. The possibility of this explosion of form was based upon a gathering development that occurred in the blue-green algae stage: the very gradual incorporation of an energy source *within* the algae, by the inclusion of other one-celled beings called mitochondria and by the symbiotic evolution of these mitochondria within their hosts ever since. The mitochondria are the energy processors for all animals, including ourselves.

The internalizing of an energy processor was an involution that later made animal mobility possible, among other benefits. Like the stars with their central energy sources, but ever so much more gentle, our cells all have these beings, the mitochondria, whose presence makes the assimilation of food useful by providing the means of extracting and using the energy that the gathered food contains.

Transition to Psyche

Let us take a leap here, bypassing the evolution of sexual reproduction, sight, and mobility, all of which were necessary and major steps on the way to self-reflexivity. We also assume the nurturing of young and the evolution of collective ways of functioning as members of a species. But let us move directly to the human level.

In chapter 2, I described the formation of the individual via interaction with others, where the real individual qualities of persons tend to come out, and by the interaction of culture-pockets (tribes). It is these differentiations of individuals from the very tight social structures that are found in these societies that first involve, or evoke, *individual-moral* feelings ("This is what I should do"), as distinct from the *social-moral* feelings ("This is the way *we* do it"). Perhaps it is an evolution from, "There is a wrongness here" to "I did something wrong" to "I chose to do that in spite of the mores, because it was right to do."

In Jung's view, with which I heartily agree, this moral dimension is at the heart of individuation. As moral differences are taken in and gathered to the consciousness of the individual, self-reflexivity arises, not just in the sense of "I do this" as distinct from "we do this," but in the real sense of differentiation of the individual from the collective. This occurs when one feels an inner directedness that can lead to actions that may actually go against the norms of the collective. This is a new light, a new involution, taking a certain individual authority inside. Perhaps the most revered example of this in American history was Henry David Thoreau, whose civil disobedience was not only conscious and responsible but had a purposive, transforming, and creative effect upon others. In its highest manifestation, such an action can be experienced as a divine calling.[5] In fact, a new layer is coming into being at the center of the psyche that is known as the Self, the archetype of wholeness and authority.

In the end, becoming free from the cultural dominants, that is, individuation, leaves one free to love humanity as a whole phenomenon, rather than just a few portions of it. Through the emergence of the individual, the unity of the whole also becomes

PHYSICAL GATHERING AND LAYERING

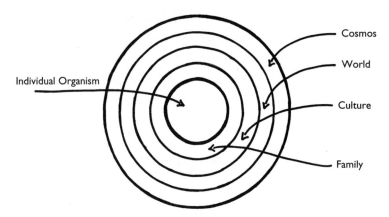

FIGURE 7.4 The layerings of the world-psyche

apparent. The individual's vision of the unity of humanity is in sharp contrast to the ethnic strife that continues to rack a world that might otherwise be civilized. I mention this because cities, the emblems of civilization, have recently been the object of destruction in, say, the former Yugoslavia, which might indeed be a part of civilization if it were not for its reversion to tribalism (Serbs vs. Croats vs. Bosnians and Albanians, etc.), which wrought such havoc there. At our stage of the evolution of consciousness, it takes many years for persons to reach the place at which such feelings of hatred and revenge are transcended. That is, it takes us humans that long to be able to see ourselves as we are now and to see what we have been in the past (which was in most cases fixed in a mindset). Seeing ourselves is rare enough, often requiring a personal disaster, but even that certainly is not one hundred percent effective in opening our eyes. But if the opening occurs, we gain the freedom to cross boundaries.

The formation of "layers" in a star during its normal evolution suggests other layerings of the world-psyche that forms our environment, as shown in figure 7.4. In the star, light is engendered. In the organism, the light of consciousness is engendered.

The whole cosmos layer is indeed there, suggesting how far we must yet evolve our consciousness and our skills to be part of the most comprehensive community.

The Ultimate Connectedness of Everything Inner and Outer

This is a good point to bring in another symbol, the hologram. A hologram is a photograph made, in principle, without the lenses that ordinarily focus light from one point in a scene to a single point on a film. Instead, the light from the whole scene reaches the whole film, so that *each point on the film contains information about the whole scene as seen from that point.*[6] The italicized portion of the last sentence is the single point about holograms that I want to bring in here, but I want to apply it by analogy to our three-dimensional cosmos instead of to a two-dimensional piece of film such as a hologram. In the previous section on the paradox of the container and the contained, I said that there is a sense in which the whole cosmos is present at each point within it, as the whole scene is present at each point of the hologram. But how might this come about? That is the topic we now approach.

A wonderful symbol of this presence of the whole at each point is the development of a fertilized ovum, whether human or that of any other animal. The DNA in each cell retains the imprint of the whole, no matter how specialized the cell. Even, say, a skin cell of an adult has the information to make a whole new adult—brain, eyes, stomach, and all—if it could be set to dividing again as the newly fertilized ovum does. The whole is present in the most remote part.

Since all possibilities in the cosmos are potentials of the patterning of hydrogen atoms, I like to emphasize that the single simplest atom is like a hologram of the cosmos. I mentioned earlier the precipitation of matter out of the energy-burst of the Big Bang.

PHYSICAL GATHERING AND LAYERING

Figure 7.5 *The diagram of the great ultimate*

In the primordial cosmic soup, although energy flows fiercely to matter and back, *the field remains unbroken,* and each particle retains the imprint of the whole. Even when particles with opposite properties are precipitated out of the energy, the opposites remain linked, so that they can recombine to a net sum of zero. The nicest symbol of this linkage is found in the Chinese yin-yang, the "diagram of the great ultimate" shown in figure 7.5.

The fact of the unbreakable linkage of opposites is represented by the dot of the opposite color in each of the two halves of the major flow.

In the point at hand, the opposites upon which we focus are the inner and the outer: there is an unbreakable link between the two, which is re-experienced by every human infant in the archaic identity of subject and object, discussed briefly in chapter 5 and in appendix 2. In some psychological systems, this phenomenon is called "infantile omnipotence," which is a good expression to use when we need to assimilate some humility, that is, when our behavior reverts to that of the infant. However, the archaic identity of subject and object refers to much more than the behavior of infants. It is with us at all times throughout our lives and includes the possibility of an experience of very mature human beings, namely, the ultimate unity of the person with the universe.

Everything outside is also inside, through our ability to take into ourselves things that increase the meaning and substance of our being and most of all because the perception of an external world is an artifact of contrast-knowledge. As Erich Neumann says:

> *Ego-consciousness represents a specifically restricted field of knowledge in which the world-continuum is broken up into constituent parts. But we must not say "into its own constituent parts," since this breaking up of the world-continuum by the conscious mind into things, attributes, and forms as separate realities which exist side by side is not even what we as total personalities directly perceive. It is the world of our ego-consciousness, artificial in a sense, that makes the world appear thus to our rationally cognizing ego. . . . We easily forget that this polarization is but a product of our cognitive system, and not a property of the world-field that forms its basis.*[7]

In the world-field, inner and outer are not distinct. Even to say that space and time become relative or distorted in extrasensory perception is to approach it from the point of view of ego-consciousness. It is rather the case that, in extrasensory perception, the world-field is more directly perceived.

As we explore both of these approaches to the unity of inner and outer, namely, that the distinction is artificial and also that we can take things in (gather), it is important to keep in mind the distinction between, and complementarity of, contrast-knowledge and field knowledge.

CHAPTER 8

Psychic Gathering and Layering

> *When the suffering has lasted long enough, so that the ego and its strength are worn down and one begins to feel one's self to be "small and ugly," then at last comes that merciful moment when reflection is possible, and the stream of energy can begin to flow back from the object toward the Self in oneself.*
>
> —MARIE-LOUISE VON FRANZ, *Projection and Recollection in Jungian Psychology*

We have seen the evolution of the physical cosmos as a process of gathering and layering, which is followed, in parallel, by the gathering and layering of organic life in the cosmos. The concentration of life in organic beings then leads to the growth of consciousness and the layering of both the conscious and unconscious sides of our being. The layers of our conscious side include our primitive knowing and later the layer in which we know that we know, which is more or less where humanity is now. And though the primitive unconscious side of the infant is quite diffuse, as we grow, it also forms a layer of unconscious material out of our personal experience, leaving the more universal layers deeper and less accessible to our ego-consciousness.

The ego is the center of the area of the individual psyche that uses contrast-knowledge, which is the ultimate goal of all science. Societies with European roots have been quite enamored of the power of the intellect to achieve contrast, and indeed that power is very great. But we have seen that contrast-knowledge is not the only kind of knowing. One example of noncontrast knowing is kinesthetic memory. In addition, there is a more direct access to some other kinds of knowing by means of the presence of the field, as introduced in the first chapter, and expanded in appendix 1.

The Self is already connected to the rest of the cosmos. We might even say the Self *is* the connection to the rest of the cosmos. What, then, is the ego for, with its contrast-knowledge? If we are already connected to everything via the Self, why bother with the arduous task of learning things? Why not just be natural? Of what use is contrast-knowledge?

Contrast-knowledge is the basis of our freedom, the fact that we can step back, form a relationship to things, and choose. It is also the source of the effectiveness of science in the use of natural laws to build things and devices that make life safer and easier. This enhances our freedom. It also makes culture possible in all of its diversity, which affords us the satisfactions of the soul through religion and the arts. With the development of consciousness, we no longer remain in a purely natural state, but we struggle against the unconsciousness of pure nature to gain our freedom. We become aware precisely of spiritual values that stand in contrast to what then can be seen as "lower" impulses. Being human becomes problematic because we begin to wonder who and what we are, a consideration that does not seem to trouble most animals, for they do not make changes in the behavior that goes with their species.

The presence of some sort of self-denial, substituting spiritual values for physical pleasures and material goods—a part of many spiritual traditions—points to the same problem of knowing who we are, though the attitudes in these traditions vary greatly. This is

PSYCHIC GATHERING AND LAYERING

consonant with one of Jung's stronger points—that the work of consciousness-building and the acquiring of freedom in the process is, in these senses, a "work against nature," or *opus contra naturam*.

As we learn things about the cosmos, in effect we assimilate it. Thus, if there is a reason for the cosmos to have evolved consciousness, *the images of the universe must be gathered to consciousness* or become accessible to the ego. This is a building process: some aspects of reality cannot even be conceived until others are already there as background. It is virtually certain that there are aspects of the cosmos that are quite inaccessible to our understanding at the present stage of our evolution.

Conscious attention is like a narrow searchlight beam that shines now on this content, now on that one, among those images and concepts that have become accessible to the ego and are associated with it. What is difficult for the ego to access (for instance, in persistent mental blocks) is what is problematic for our seeing and understanding. A mindset that "sees" evolution excludes one that "sees" creationism, and vice versa. The attitudes behind them are also mutually exclusive. The ego can be closed to an image for other reasons as well, including a differently oriented talent, or wounds experienced in one's personal history, or cultural baggage, which blocks the opening of the ego's immediate access area. The searchlight image is good because such a light produces the contrasts of which we have been speaking.

We now are going to look at our involvement with, and assimilation of, the cosmos itself from a different perspective from that of chapter 5, which will extend the parallels of gathering and layering that have now been developed. Here, the heart-re-envisioning focuses on the cosmos as the totality of psychic images that can be taken within by the individual. The dissolving of the rigidity of the separation of inner and outer, upon which we have been working, now makes this possible and desirable.

Gathering Consciousness

The discussion that follows is based largely on material found in Marie-Louise von Franz's wonderful book, *Projection and Recollection in Jungian Psychology: Reflections of the Soul.*[1] What she calls "recollection" is the aspect of gathering that we are now considering. We will approach this topic from a "how we know that it is so" standpoint. First let us look at the individual. Later we can describe the origin of consciousness in the human species by a process of gathering out of the archaic identity (chapter 5) or out of the field.

Consciousness arises as we gradually develop more and more accurate images of the world and of ourselves as part of that world. From an adult point of view, an infant is quite mistaken in its infantile omnipotence. From its own limited point of view, however, its attitude is quite effective, but for reasons that it does not understand. When it cries, it gets attention but not because it actually possesses godlike power. Generally, the growing child must learn many lessons as to the nature of the world before it achieves the freedom that it desires. Once the child realizes that much power is external to itself, that is, that there are powers other than itself, the process can take root: the more we learn of the world, the more power for freedom we acquire.[2]

Our adult realization as to how archaic identity operates comes through the fact that the growth of consciousness involves continual corrections to our understanding and our attitude. This alerts us to the presence of a general process. In psychological terms, we project our ideas or assumed realities onto the environment, and as long as they "work," there is no need for adjustment.

In *The Archetypes and the Collective Unconscious,* Jung defined projection as an unperceived and unintentional, that is, unconscious, transfer of subjective psychic contents onto an outer object.[3] As noted above, this is our primordial and natural state. Jung also says:

> *Unless we are possessed of an unusual degree of self-awareness, we shall never see through our projections but must always succumb to them, because the mind in its natural state presupposes the reality of such projections.*[4]

Often a whole segment of a culture practices the same ideas, in which case we could say that that whole group is projecting. If, for example, one is a member of a community that shares a belief that the cosmos was created six thousand years ago and if one stays within that group, then everyone whom one asks about this topic will substantiate the belief. In this case, we could say that people in the group have a worldview that is illusory from another point of view, say, that of scientific evidence. But it is not simply that such a view can be "corrected" on the basis of evidence, for such evidence is not authoritative for the person we are considering. We find that the whole being and identity of the person are very strongly linked to the idea in question. This is the evidence of projection, which signifies some sort of archaic identity of subject and environment.

But where do mythic ideas concerning the cosmos come from? One might say, from a sacred text, but ultimately even these arise within human beings. Even the current (at whatever era) ideas within the scientific community have a mythic component. The difference is in the means that science uses for evolving those ideas, namely, sophisticated technological observation and experimentation, yielding further evidence.

Through the phenomenon of archaic identity, one believes that the world really is a certain way. And so it is, until a conflict arises on the basis of that assumption. More importantly, *unless a conflict arises, we will remain unconscious even of much of what we assume the world to be like.* That is, using again our example concerning the date of the creation of the world, we can have a definite idea, or we can have no conscious idea at all in cases about which we have done no reflection and still run into the tenacity of identity when the subject comes up. We can see that there have been such assumptions in human history, for our example is based on fact. What is always less clear to us is that there still continues to be a virtually inexhaustible store of unconscious assumptions, that is, projections, and each of us, no matter how well read, still abounds with unchallenged assumptions.

Von Franz gives the example of how children invest their toys, such as dolls and airplanes, with life and reality. She notes that the child has some consciousness that the toy is inanimate but makes the important point that parents can no longer "join unaffectedly in play of this kind, because their conviction that the doll, say, is inanimate and the parent-child game is *only fantasy* hinders them in acting out the game."[5] This observation gives us the needed contrast between the adult's point of view and that of the child.

In cultures such as ancient Greece, "the whole world was alive with demons and spirits."[6] This sort of animism is well recognized as belonging to earlier periods of many cultures. And yet a higher form of this investment gives much of poetry its power. The feelings that we get in nature, and the symbolic resonance of such things as storms, the rising and setting of the sun and the moon, the realities of deserts and jungles, and so much more, are a part of our very being at home on the planet. Life consists of these things and is at the same time symbolically reflected in them in an irreducible link.

When we transcend our worldviews, we do so by seeing nature more deeply, taking nature in: gathering. Our mistake is that every time a worldview is transcended, we believe that it has been displaced by the final correct answer! What this does psychologically is simply to restore the original archaic identity whereby we believe that the world *really is a certain way,* and we lose our consciousness of the fact that this view will also be found wanting at some future time. We lose contact with the unknown, which is the source of the mysterious symbolic ties we have with nature.

We also need to be aware of how the archaic identity of subject and object works in interpersonal relations. About this, von Franz comments that our unconscious assumption that the other person functions and thinks in the same manner that we do induces us to try to improve others. This is often a substitute for improving ourselves. If we recognized the "defects" that we assume belong to others are really our own and that we can only grow in consciousness by taking ownership of our flaws, we would be more compassionate. As von Franz says, "This difficult moral task makes it impossible for any relatively conscious person to want to improve other people and the world."[7]

This is the basis for a true human pluralism on our planet.

In an appendix, I have put a descriptive table showing the cyclic nature of gathering in contents of the cosmos for consciousness and the reestablishment of archaic identity. The central idea, however, is the following, so I will risk repeating it. Usually, when we make a discovery, whether in science or any other field, we say something like: "Aha! So that's the way things *really* are!" *This statement is precisely a reassertion of the archaic identity of subject and object.* Insofar as a new discovery, either scientific or personal, is seen as a final truth, the way things *really* are, we are back at the beginning, identifying the cosmos with what we *think* it is, just like the child living from infantile omnipotence, though on a more sophisticated level. But there is now, and always will be, more of ourselves, as well as more of the cosmos, to see and assimilate.

A new discovery may well enhance our stability and control of events, but it may in addition enchain our mind with illusion, if we treat it as fixed and final. What it requires of us is that we finally see that there is no final seeing, that we are not excused by our progress from further progress, that we are still and always *called into being.*

Our education in this matter is simultaneously a leading out of the true heart of the individual, and a taking in of the whole cosmos by the same person. The total process amounts to a meeting. It is also felt as a journey both going outward and returning; finding ourselves is finding a home for God within our own being. Sheila Moon put it thus in her poem *The Herder:*

> *My loud-voiced fearful heart*
> *has not gone to its knees*
> *enough before that insistent Herder*
> *who writes runes, queer and sharp,*
> *across all wander-ways of sheep.*
> *A needing lamb, my heart stumbles*
> *and falls and cannot further*
> *go and feels bereft of the flock*
> *and lost and lost and lost.*
> *But the Herder knows weft*
> *and warp of woven life where*
> *all roads part and cross and part,*
> *knows that being left alone*
> *is risk, is loss large enough*
> *to push lambs to their feet and*
> *onward to find the gate unlocked*
> *to sheepfold, with a hush*
> *of sanctuary for all hearts*
> *that have dared terror to the bone*
> *and given thanks and taken hold*
> *of faintest path and followed.*
> *The Herder is very old and knows that*
> *a choice to go whatever way—*
> *rough, smooth, above, below—*
> *if it is choice from courage*
> *it leads a heart home.*[8]

PSYCHIC GATHERING AND LAYERING

For each movement of the heart and life, both directions of energy flow, inward and outward, apply in complete aptness. In the taking in of the cosmos, energy "streams back" to the individual psyche and "flows outward" in new living. The very difficulty of assigning a fixed direction of flow to this process shows its truth value because it is a holding of opposites that reflects the reality. There is always that in the world that leads the heart outward, but the heart remains inward, and, as noted, the very process of going out is self-discovery that "leads a heart home." This is our experience. The courage to be is the courage both to "come out" with one's true heart, risking its vulnerability for the sake of humanity, and at the same time to "let the world in," with the same risk.

By this process we gain both our contrast-knowledge and our consciousness.

Hidden in our surroundings are fragments of the Divine. We encountered this idea earlier in chapter 5, in the quotation from the Gnostic text by von Franz, in which God says to the prophetess, "I am scattered in all things" and declares to her that gathering herself and gathering God are identical.[9] That which is mutually gathered is encompassed in Jung's term, the Self, the god-image in the individual and the individual's more complete personhood. However, the ego needs to be formed, and one is usually protected from too early an encounter with the Divine. Not every life fulfills the preparations for such encounters. We can remain unaware of the inner presence of the Self. Many of us find the spiritual dimension deepening in us in the second half of life. Even so, the process may be largely unconscious, for the Self can only speak to us through what we have already assimilated of the world.

All of the external things that attract us could be seen as pieces of the Divine calling us, if we were awake. What do we really want through money, gadgets, and games? Behind all of that, we seek aliveness, and we fail to find it. Spiritual movement is replaced by whatever it is in these things that moves us—or by the impact of art on us or whatever it is we choose. Nevertheless, we all are still seeking something: our selves and God. It takes a long and varied life to come to the realization that we have been in love with our egos instead.

The Self is calling us to ourselves—not to the ego, but to the greater being we might become, with the givens of our lives, in accordance with the teleonomic view that we contain our own free destiny. The process of getting past ourselves to love another also applies to the other value-objects as well. Only when we cease to love ourselves in the object can we begin to see and love things in the world for themselves. Only when the ego has gained enough of consciousness by accepting the hints of the Self can it sacrifice its claim to priority to gain the final freedom of living from a greater whole without worrying about material survival.

Only the greatest mystics have had a more-or-less direct access to their own inner worlds. The rest of us see by reflection and by noting our feeling-response to things in our environment, that is, by taking stock of and owning our projections. The ego learns ways of defending against this recognition. Figure 8.1 is a diagram of typical ego-defenses, with respect to things external and things within. The Self is here portrayed as the central layer or core, as before, and the ego is portrayed as occupying a small portion of the periphery of the person, as in the searchlight image used earlier.

We mostly think of projection as a defense against insight. However, it is generally also the only possibility of new insight, because it is, as just brought out, the Self's primary means of communication with the ego. The collapse of a projection is always a painful lesson for the ego, but without this pain there can be no growth in consciousness. After all, defenses have their evolutionary value, too. When they are out of date, however, they become destructive in themselves.

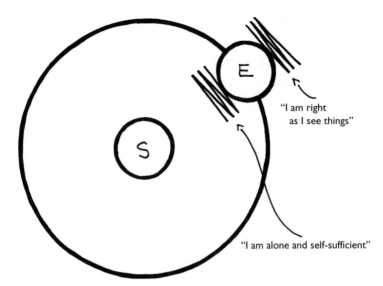

FIGURE 8.1 *The ego's defensive slogans*

When the ego perceives something new, it feels the energy transfer, the resonance of what is new with what is known. But the ego is also required to learn how to respond creatively to new situations, how to let the Self, which has a greater comprehensiveness, lead the way.

The Self is the representative of the field in the individual (and beyond), and the field and its patterning shape the whole cosmos in its early evolution. The capacity of the Self for shaping so-called external things can be seen in its ability to produce synchronistic events, which are, by the way, attempts to get the attention and commitment of the ego, which is not merely a yielding of the ego but its recognition and participation in the deeper process that was always at work in the individual life.[10]

The field is unbroken, though contrast-knowledge has attempted to separate the inner and the outer: one can only take the whole cosmos inside because it *is* inside and not only symbolically. Inside and outside are relative in the field. To speak of retrieving the energy that has been devoted to projection is to speak of letting the energy flow from the Self within, from the heart of the cosmos, from the heart of God. It is to give voice to the Voice.[11]

The Role of Symbols

We have a deep inward knowledge of the insight quoted from the Christian church father Origen in chapter 4, namely, that "we" are scattered about in our own environment or, what is the same thing, that everything outside ourselves belongs inside. He also said that, in gathering ourselves, we gather God. If we say that this is a symbolic statement, we must again remember that inner and outer have only relative reality. There is indeed a concrete world, but to speak of it as wholly identical with the outer world is wrong and is only the point of view of contrast-knowledge. As we "take in" the cosmos, not with mere intellectual understanding but in our living, the change renders God more effective within us, as Origen said. When I say "in our living," I mean that we really consent to be a part of the cosmos *as it is,* which means that we are open in love with something essentially unknown. In a life truly lived, one is inwardly attuned to outward actions. It is the symbol that unites the two. As Jung said, the symbolic life is the meaningful life.[12] A life composed of exterior facts alone is not worth mentioning.

The infant is analogous to the ungathered cosmos. In a sense, we might picture God scattered like the dots in figure 7.1a, the first "gathering" diagram of the ungathered cosmos, if we visualize the dots as symbols of value, or carriers of meaning, as some mystics have said God is scattered in each of us. The dots are also all those things outside ourselves onto which we project value and meaning.[13] What might it be that would gather all the fragments of God not only from the remote places of the earth but also from the

PSYCHIC GATHERING AND LAYERING

depths of cosmic space? What I picture is something like their own psychic gravity, to use gravity as an analogy. In *The Origin and History of Consciousness*, Erich Neumann called this phenomenon "centroversion."[14] It is empirical, which is to say, it happens. The infant begins to gather the universe in learning about the world, about self and other, but the universe is really gathering itself to form the person. How far the person will go in self-integration cannot be predicted.

To recapitulate, our journey of this chapter began in chapter 7, where we first saw the spirit-matter points in figure 7.1 brought together by physical gravity. Those points of spirit-matter are really symbols in the sense that they do actually contain all the potentials of the cosmos, as the material on holograms emphasized. These potentials include our possible God-realization, as well as all that will follow us in virtually endless time.

The next use of the gathering diagram, figure 7.3, was at the level of planetary soup, where life molecules gather into living organisms. No consciousness of divine will attends this stage of evolution, but it also is nonetheless a step in the God-gathering.

The infant, too, is ungathered. Though the infant is a concrete person with unique givens, that child is also quite similar to the diagram, in the sense that the newborn person is completely diffuse psychologically, as he/she is physically. The difference is that there is now this specific being to act as a psychic "gravitational" center for the gathering of the meaning of *this* life.

That meaning will not manifest itself in a life completely detached from its environment. In one sense, the meaning of life is all "inside," but what is inside can never be discovered except through exploration of the environment and the other beings in it. This is the message of education, to be sure, but we must apply it even more deeply if we are to come to terms with the religious dimension of our lives. We cannot stop with mere education in any usual sense. Behind the true heart, which is the outcome of being led out, is the heart of God, which makes possible a much deeper fulfillment than simply being oneself.

The aspect of the Self as a center of completeness, or a locus of symbolic gathering, is present even in the hydrogen atom, which itself manifests *mandala* (wholeness) symbolism.[15] In this sense, the Self is present in every configuration of atoms from the very beginning. This, again, is the hologram of the cosmos. What is new in the infant is a more highly evolved personal God-center, which is the fruit of evolution of our species and an especially effective "organ" for the gathering of symbolic meaning. The gathering occurs, again, in terms of personal meaning, without which living is despair. A gathering in terms of meaning is not possible for creatures without ego-consciousness. So, in a diagram of the infant as gathering center, we would not have mere diffuseness, but a new instrument for consciousness: a Self that is at once potently organized and attractive, which also contains the archetypes that it has gathered in the course of the evolution of the species.

The ego is not present at birth, though some of the givens of the personality, such as extraversion or introversion, are seen very early in childhood. The ego is built up by living those experiences that differentiate the "I" from the "not-I," especially those that strengthen the concreteness of the outer world. The outer world is stable and completely convincing. It must be, for it alone provides the ultimate conditions of freedom, as I have shown.

In figure 7.3b, a dotted circle symbolizes the new organism. But the symbols are not so much gathered *to* the Self, the center of the circle, as they are used *by* the Self to build ego-consciousness. In this process, the Self shows or reveals itself to the ego by showing it not just religious symbols but the whole cosmos, with its light and dark sides. Again, we think of the quotation from *The Gospel of Eve,* in which God speaks to the prophetess:

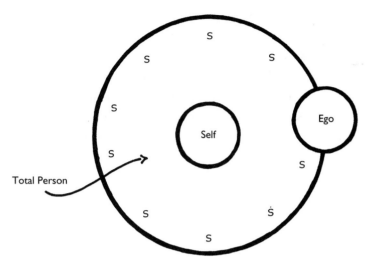

FIGURE 8.2 *Gathering of symbols (S)*

I am thou, and thou art I, and wherever thou art, there am I, and I am scattered in all things, and from wherever thou wilt thou canst gather me, but in gathering me thou gatherest thyself.[16]

This is all consistent. In figure 8.1 above, the person is shown as a circle, within which the ego moves about in its searchlight function. The symbols that it gathers, shown by the Self, gather in the periphery of the person, in that area accessible to the ego (see figure 8.2).

In this process, the person becomes more and more a carrier of Self qualities, for the symbols are not there just as a sort of treasure store but affect the daily living of the one who has become more conscious.

Ungathered symbols blind as well as enlighten, for, as noted above, we have difficulty in seeing that it is indeed the Self at work. Usually we take the symbolic object at the face value of its attractiveness before recognizing that something is trying to communicate with us through it. While a particular symbol is active, one needs no more, no further awakening, for the active symbol grants a sufficient sense of having been awakened. Great ideas are symbols that channel the energy of great numbers of people, weld societies, and transform cultures. Examples are monotheism, monogamy, human equality, capitalism, communism, liberation of the oppressed, the apocalyptic view, the Word, the great person, and science. Not all of these last as values.

Channeling Energy

This seems to be the place to mention another idea of great importance: the conversion of mere energy-flow into "work." We have already encountered the notion that the development of consciousness is an *opus contra naturam,* a labor against nature, and the same idea is amplified in what follows.

We may picture a waterfall for the image of the natural energy flow. Let it be one that is beautiful to look at but whose water could be diverted by conscious intention to flow through a turbine to produce needed electrical energy, which might then be used to enhance the quality of living. Thus a conflict of values arises, as has occurred in assessing the future of many watercourses in the United States in recent years. One value is the experience of nature, while the other is power for manufacturing and ease of living. Work, in the sense of this image (developed by Jung), is *intentionally channeled energy.* The flow is beautiful, while the work is the foundation of culture, which is also beautiful. Or rather, this is one way to look at it. The truth is that some energy flows, in nature and also in us, are violent and dangerous as well as sometimes awesomely beautiful. Our negative projections sometimes release energy flows of the violent and dangerous kind. It is natural flow, a form of untamed psychic energy. Our acculturation to the reality of other persons demands of us that we find ways to channel this energy and put it to work in other ways. Our projections, if clung to after they have served their initial purpose of making us aware that the quality we have reacted to in the other is really our own, become just an excuse for our emotionalism with regard to the things that "bug" us. These waterfalls, or torrents, are not beautiful, except in the cases where an individual is just beginning to overcome inhibitions to the expression of anger.

We certainly would not want to turn every waterfall in nature to "useful" purposes, but we also want to raise our quality of living beyond mere subsistence. To what extent the channeling of flow into work should be undertaken, and the timing of such efforts, varies with each individual case. I want only to point out the paradoxical pull of the two values.

There is perhaps an analogy here of the creation of the cosmos in the Big Bang as God's work: somehow energy is channeled into the form that we now know as spirit-matter. In the hot dense point of being that the new cosmos was, something that I have called the Patterning channeled energy into material forms (quarks and leptons), drawing upon the structure of the energy field to do so. Did that process have a goal of producing conscious and spiritual beings?

All we can say is that the seed of such beings certainly was present. That is, there was not necessarily a goal on the part of a being external to the process itself. Therefore, this is not *teleological* but *teleonomic,* the difference being that the goal is not external but carried internally, with freedom to evolve in many possible ways. Although I have been stressing the relativity of inner and outer, it is of the greatest importance here to work at owning the inwardness, as part of assimilating the cosmos.

Symbols are energy regulators. The only way to gain the energy source that has been developed through the symbol is, in the end, to *see through* the symbol. But this can only be done by finding (encountering) a new symbol with a strong enough pull on us to displace the previous one. At the same time, this requires a deeper factuality, for facts are powerfully transformative, enabling or forcing us to see what we could not see previously. The new fact reveals the new symbol. In the religious tradition in which I grew up, Jesus was not only Christ, but the One God of Heaven and Earth. To me, this was a symbol of great power. I worked to understand it and to live a life "worthy" of it. Then I attended seminars that undertook a critical study of the synoptic Gospels and discovered, through the evidence in the comparison of texts, that Jesus' self-estimate did not include being "the Christ."[17] At the same time, what Jesus did teach, according to my gathering of evidence, was of tremendously greater depth than the teachings I had encountered in my upbringing. This was the real key to the symbol that has turned me in the direction of my present work, and it embodies all the elements that I have just described.

Humans under the influence of any symbol that has brought forth the present state but which is obstructive to further development are still serving what they believe in an altruistic fashion. The only ethical manner in which to influence their action is by gently leading them toward facts that are discordant with their views, to shift the energy flow into the newer channel, while simultaneously supporting the grief-work in relation to the old symbol. All of this is provided they are seeking our help, which sometimes happens. And it may not work. It is only what one discovers for oneself that becomes a ground for lasting change.

Is love symbolic? Or is it, perhaps, the *medium* of symbol formation? If the child is treated with love, the true heart opens out. Insofar as people respond to the gift of love with reciprocal devotion, love is indeed symbolic. On the other hand, insofar as love need not be transcended, it is not symbolic. The key, perhaps, is that some "loves" do in fact need to be let go and left behind.

Love is relevant to the transformative gathering process, and

PSYCHIC GATHERING AND LAYERING

lies behind all of our desires, wanting us to see it more clearly in its own right. Since each of us is the locus of a God-center, interpersonal love is of the greatest value to the process.

How does one treat people with love, so that the love is perceived through the pain of becoming? Here the Golden Rule is the key but not in the usual interpretation. The text says that whatever we desire that others do toward us we ought to do toward them. I have heard Christian clergy recoil in horror at this rule, saying that it gives license to any mutually consenting behavior whatsoever, but that is not how I read it. To me, it makes us ask ourselves as deeply as possible what it is that we really do want. We want to be recognized, valued, and loved. Much of the time what we think we want, especially in the area of gratification, comes from our woundedness. In our depths, we want healing, forgiveness, and freedom from unchosen dangers. To treat other humans as having value is to honor the highest potential in each one. Let me be perfectly clear that what is my highest potential may well be unconscious to me. I am referring only to a general desire for myself and the other that we may bring forth the fullness of our being. Someone who loves another will put forth a great effort to turn him or her aside from self-destructive behavior, because that is indeed what they would desire from the true heart that another would do for them. With reflection, we can see possibilities for using the flow of love for the mutual benefit of ourselves and others. To me, this feels equivalent to love's desire to be so used. This feeling has led many to absurd uses of energy. As I see the Golden Rule, what we desire is neither comfort nor mere pleasure or avoidance of pain but something of the highest possible value, through choice that is conscious of such values. We can only value things in relation to the breadth of our knowledge of the world and of the cosmos.

The Self, while it must be evoked from and expressed through the individual, encompasses the whole cosmos. This fact continually forces us to broaden our perspective. There are indeed love relationships among humans, which is where we are and where we begin. People are concrete. We need each other. This is both in and from the Self that encompasses the whole.

But Earth is also evolving, and the beings who have evolved upon the planet find themselves incomplete and not only in relation to nearby humans. They feel incomplete which is to say that the incompleteness is a symbol in itself. This is the state of perpetual disequilibrium; this is life. Many of us are gathering-in more and more of the whole earth as never before and not only her diverse peoples but all of her endangered processes and being.

What the cosmos apparently lacks is precisely what God *is:* love, love of the whole. The creation of a cosmos wherein finite beings must gather the whole (and respond to its woundedness) for the sake of consciousness is the only vehicle for the Self-realization of love. This is the image of the Kingdom of God.

CHAPTER 9

Integrating

> *The cosmos could not possibly be explained as a dust of unconscious elements, on which life, for some incomprehensible reason, burst into flower. . . . It is fundamentally and primarily living, and its complete history is ultimately nothing but an immense psychic exercise. . . . From this point of view humanity is nothing but the point of emergence in nature, at which this deep cosmic evolution declares itself. . . . Humanity is the flame of a general fermentation of the universe which breaks out suddenly on the earth.*
>
> —Pierre Teilhard de Chardin, *Human Energy*

Re-envisioning the universe with the heart is understanding it with our feeling, seeing how it serves the ultimate richness of life, and finally entering into its process as participants. The cosmos re-envisioned with the heart is the cosmos as home. Being at home is one profound meaning of integration and shows in yet another way that the heart-vision is primary.

The heart-essence of the universe lies in the reality of freedom, love, consciousness, and meaning, as reflected in a relatively small number of primary aspects: it is creative, evolutionary, gathering, transformative, emerging, individuating, integrating, healing, and beautiful. These are the qualities out of which our home is built.

All of these aspects are process-oriented. They are what the cosmos does because it is fundamentally in disequilibrium and must keep evolving. With each of these aspects, the process involves an opening up and communicating across boundaries.

Here again we will draw parallels—this time, parallels with the integrating aspect of the overall process at all stages of evolution thus far considered. Our purpose is to show integration as an aspect of the universe. This integration might be called *building the heart of the cosmos*. Integration can occur on all levels, from the individual through the group, the culture, and the planet, and onward to the whole cosmos. The means by which peoples and cultures are integrated into the cosmos, however, lie in the integration of individuals into ever-wider areas of life.

The integration of an individual as a person, which can be approached but never finally realized, involves the person's assimilating as much of the cosmos as possible into the way in which that person lives. That is, individuals lead the way toward the integration of the life of the planet and beyond. The process of becoming oneself as a unique person, which builds consciousness, ultimately serves the integration of the cosmos, for unconscious wholeness is incomplete. Only a conscious wholeness holds meaning.

The microcosm, the individual who is consciously linked to the whole, thus not only reflects the macrocosm, as the ancients recognized, but also completes it. While we thus cannot rest within an original unbroken wholeness, the need to be completed through consciousness poses problems for integration because the holding together of the great opposites of living, such as heart and mind, masculine and feminine, self and other, and individual and community, becomes an issue. We can only find wholeness living in the midst of contrasts and only by accepting the demand and reality of each pole of the issues involved.

Only a cosmos that manifests opposites or contradictions can be a cosmos on the way to completeness. Only in a wounded cosmos is healing meaningful. Healing is the essence of integration. This is the theme that will be developed as the book comes to a close: *the universe sets problems that only love can solve,* for every healing manifests love in some way. Thus, the universe engenders love—brings it forth amid all of its living potentials as the integrating thread that weaves all into a whole. Because wholeness includes both members of each pair of opposites, a universe in process of realizing its inherent wholeness must *necessarily* set problems that only love can solve.

What is Integration?

Integration is any process that furthers integrity or unity of being, on any level of cosmic evolution. Gravity integrates stars individually as it also integrates the whole physical cosmos. Gravity provides a wonderful analogy with love, for it is the only one of the four physical forces that manifests an attraction of everything in the cosmos for everything else. The other forces repel as well as attract. Since I spoke earlier of the fact that gravity causes the fundamental disequilibrium (open-ended evolution) of the cosmos, the analogy would suggest that love ultimately moves all the processes in the universe.

The formation of cell walls serves the integrity of life-processes within, as does the skin of any evolved being with respect to the functioning of its characteristic life. Something diverse is held together for complex and creative functioning—a functioning that nonetheless exhibits a unity and a beauty in that unity. The cell gives us a model for our own holding together of all the opposites of our lives, but what is easy as unconscious living becomes difficult when consciousness is at issue.

For humans, in particular, unity of being seems to entail

considerable difficulty. Rabbi Abraham J. Heschel observed that, while a horse has no problem being a horse, being a human is definitely a problem for humans.[1] Perhaps this is because both wholeness and consciousness are involved. The horse has wholeness, undisturbed by self-reflexivity. Many humans settle unconsciously into forms of existence that give the appearance of unity but do so on the basis of a partial manifestation of that individual's potentials. These forms usually manifest collective values rather than consciously acquired ones. People tend to avoid contradictions and problems in living.

One way we do this is to identify with various things, such as a job, a social position, a nationality, or a race. Or, we happily do those things that all those around us are doing: building toward retirement; having a hobby; being knowledgeable about entertainment, wines, etc., even in a highly refined manner. We then can be "open," and aware of being open, but only in certain well-traveled areas, while remaining unaware of the uncrossed boundaries and secret fears. We are "okay" because our neighbors are just the same as we are. Integration, however, involves the crossing of boundaries in a consistent process of continuing to expand our horizons.

The horse is a whole horse, and biologically we are whole humans. Conscious wholeness, or integration, is a new problem for us because there is in principle no limit to our potential for expansion, in either psychological or spiritual terms. Only the emergence of consciousness opens this door. As our biological wholeness is regulated by DNA and such, our psychological and spiritual wholeness, both as individuals and as a species, is regulated by the central archetype, the Self, as documented by Jung.

Three keywords of integration are *openness, communication,* and the *dissolving* of boundaries. Openness is needed for the inclusion of what we lack for our completeness. Communication also requires openness but also involves interactions with other humans and the rest of nature, the building of a world community, and the sense of Earth as home. That is, the wholeness of individuals rests upon the diversity of humanity and of the world. Our own unity is gradually defined by means of subtle contrasts found in the entire human field. Whether or not the dissolution of external boundaries is needed depends on the individual case; but we never know ourselves fully, and there are always boundaries within that are difficult to cross.

Interlude: Reflections on Cultural Boundaries

Our main focus is on integration at the individual level because that is a prerequisite for the true integration of groups, cultures, and planets. However, cultures do not always readily accept the impact that open individuals have on them.

A person who has experienced multiple cultures is not upset by being a guest among them but can maintain whatever identity he or she has chosen in life, remaining a true individual, true to a unique set of personal values. But cultures show great instabilities when they make the transition from isolation to openness, for their members have not necessarily developed this kind of resilience. This may mean that a given culture has a lack of wholeness that will prove damaging to its attempt to become an open and functioning part of a world community.

One example of lack of wholeness is a cultural subgroup that experiences less actual freedom than another subgroup. The Soviet Union apparently held some of the forces of ethnic reaction in check without actually fostering the evolution toward an attitude of citizenship of the whole; as the new millennium begins, we are still seeing the terrified reaction to the attempt to open cultural boundaries in many parts of the former Communist world. This reaction takes the form of ethnic clashes. We may also see this occur in China as well, when communication grows somewhat from its present level. In the United States, though we have laws against discrimination of various sorts, it remains the case that members of one group fear to enter the territory of another, which would not be the case if all of us achieved the wholeness of humanity within ourselves.

Once the boundaries of a culture are opened for a time, it probably can be seen what parts of that culture constitute a true cultural individuality that can stand against influences from other parts of the globe. Europe is an example of a unified region within which separate cultures can be maintained. Japan is willy-nilly assimilating some "Western" cultural influences that at present are disturbing what it has been. The difference is that Japan has had less time than Western countries to interact and find its true identity within the world community. Some Middle Eastern countries have tried to maintain the subordination of women while attempting to communicate and trade with European nations. It seems unlikely that oppression of women can last as a tradition in a modernizing state, though the transition may well be quite protracted. The men of those countries would at present say of me that I "just don't understand," though the women are beginning to be heard from, and their actions and demands seem to indicate that I do.

The point is that real communication tends to initiate a sifting of values and the raising of consciousness.

The integration of the earth with other civilizations in the galaxy and in the cosmos beyond is likely far off in the future. Humans have devoted considerable energy already to the possible modeling of what earthlings might find when they become spacefarers and begin to contact the network of civilizations from planets of other stars. Futurists have speculated as to what sorts of communications and "regional" galactic libraries there might be, for there is a high probability that such things already exist, and we will be latecomers to the community. However, the reality will probably surprise us.

Openness, communication, and the dissolving of those boundaries, cultural and psychological, that block our seeing and perpetuate lack of wholeness lead us toward the heart of our integration as human beings. This integration is really the reunification of opposites in living, among which are our inner and outer worlds and our spirit and matter sides. I say *re*unification because the opposites are created for us in the process of forming the ego, as described in chapter 8. The opposites are real enough, though they remain interpretations of a total reality that always retains an ultimately unknown quality. There are many pairs of opposites with which we must contend in our lives, and in many respects, our inner geography resembles a map of the world, divided into conflicting enclaves. At least this is the case until we begin the journey of inner exploration and also begin to hold the reins of communication among the diverse inner parts.

Integration in Relation to Earlier Themes

First, I would like to relate the theme of integration to some of the themes presented earlier. In chapter 1, the Anthropic Principle was outlined, which says that the physical nature of a universe in which living beings arise by evolution must be such that living beings *can* arise. Beyond mere physical life, the beings we observe on our planet also possess a growing capacity for consciousness and indeed for spirituality. These, too, must be a potential of the whole physical cosmos as spirit-matter. They must be "permitted" by the nature of the evolving "stuff of the universe," as Teilhard de Chardin called it.[2] Should we then call our cosmos a *human* universe? Although humanity is a concept sufficiently large that we have difficulty encompassing it in our lives, it is undoubtedly too small for the cosmos as a whole.

The Anthropic Principle holds deep implications for, or places constraints upon, the nature of the evolving "stuff." It must have a capacity for freedom and internalization, just for starters. As spirit-matter, the atoms of an anthropic universe must in fact be elementary freedoms. The freedom inherent in atoms is possible because "matter," that is, spirit-matter, has inherent contradictions in its makeup as seen from a rational viewpoint. It cannot be rationalistically defined or described. Its nature cannot be made rationally clear. *Thus we are forced to interpret and continually reinterpret what this "stuff" is.* It would be impossible to overstate the importance of this point or the value of being forced continually to reinterpret nature. In these interpretations, we invest the cosmos with meaning, but the fact that we do this means that meaning is found in the cosmos and is an inherent potential of spirit-matter. It does not detract from meaning in any way to say that it is a projection of ours, for we are a product of the evolution of the cosmos.

If meaning is manifest in and through our consciousness, so be it! Some have looked upon the cosmos and found its essence meaningless. Some have taken the opposite path. Since the contradictions are contradictions *as seen by us* in our contrast-knowledge, it is up to us how we relate to this "stuff," what *Weltanschauung* (worldview) we come to in response to the cosmos. Contradictions in the nature of physical reality imply choice on the part of those who perceive them as such. It cannot be overemphasized that inherent contradictions yield freedom, as well as being the source of wounds! Contradictions are what we bump up against, forcing us to choose in relation to opposites.

As it is always my goal to find the models for human action inhering in the potentials of the stuff of the universe, I want to show the basis for working with opposites here.

Our understanding of nature grows as we discover and attempt to resolve its contradictions. The approach to this resolution can follow either of two paths. The first is an "either/or" choice, while the second is the holding or balancing of the two opposites. Both approaches, if appropriately applied, are necessary to completeness in integration. The word *resolve* is marvelously ambiguous, for, in rationalistic terms, it means to choose one of two opposites as correct, whereas psychologically it refers to settling on a course of action.

For the past three hundred years, the ideal has been that of logical resolution; but in this century, we have finally come up against contradictions in physical reality for which logical resolution is impossible—in which the appropriate attitude is that of holding the opposites. This situation is known in physics as "complementarity." Physicist Edward Teller described it as follows:

> *The idea of complementarity is that in order to describe a situation you have to use (at least on certain occasions) two mutually exclusive approaches. If you omit either, the description is incomplete. Both must be used. Because they are mutually exclusive, it is necessary to adjust the two approaches in a manner that is by no means obvious.*[3]

In physics, as in our lives, there are cases in which opposites, that is, contradictions, are each quite necessary to a complete description of a situation. I want to stress the latter part of the quotation, however—that the balance or adjustment is "by no means obvious." There is, in fact, no rational way to adjust two logically contradictory approaches that are both needful, only a practical way that is effective in a given, unique situation. Logic always must exclude one of two such elements. Therefore, since rationality holds no key, we are free in the matter. In all of those frequent cases in which we cannot make rational adjustments to bring opposites into logical alignment, what most stands to our aid is resolve, in the sense of "fortitude." We need fortitude to hold both opposites as we can, a fortitude born of love.

The biblical case of Solomon proposing to divide the baby and give half to each of the two claimants seems to portray the play of opposites and the kind of wisdom we need in relating to them in the situation. One woman said, "Fine, let the baby be neither hers nor mine," but the true mother came to light when she said, "No, give the child to her, but let it live." In this case, both Solomon and the mother showed the fortitude born of love, to hold opposite possibilities in suspension.

We expect to encounter problems that only love can solve in a cosmos evolving from elementary freedoms, a cosmos whose roots do not yield to rational disentangling. That an example such as that of Solomon's judgment occurs is an application of the Anthropic Principle. We also know such situations in our lives; one is the difficulty of applying both mercy and justice either in law or in some interpersonal wounding. We now find that physical stuff holds the same structure, the embodiment of opposites, which can be seen as the root of our human freedom.

But let us look at it the other way around. If such is the nature of physical reality, the implication is that we can understand why freedom is more embodied the more contradictions are perceived and engaged in our living. None of us has eliminated all unconsciously held contradictions from our lives, as our friends know well. Nor can we work with our contradictions until we are able to see them. Thus our unconsciousness binds us, and consciousness, taking a creative relationship to the opposites in our lives, epitomizes freedom.

The connection has also been drawn between freedom and individuality, which is the hallmark of creativity.[4] Since the universe is the perceived and interpreted universe, we actually live in as many cosmoi as there are interpretations of it. Each of us has a freedom to interpret the cosmos, that is, to create the cosmos we live in, including what we believe is real and important; but we also live in the cosmos as conceived by each other person whom we encounter. True, we often forget that the other's universe is different from ours and offend the other by crossing boundaries that do not exist in our interpretation but do in the other's. We behave as if the cosmos is exactly and only what we each think it is. In other words, there are virtually as many cosmoi as there are sentient beings in it.

Though I have been insisting that there is no final correct interpretation of the cosmos, it is still true that the cosmos-in-itself must be one and whole, eternally unfolding from within itself. This points to a central problem of integration, for the development of factual knowledge in scientific endeavor has the effect of increasing the agreement of worldviews in a broad segment of humanity. In my work, I am attempting to increase the potential for such agreement. Here I am stressing the factual knowledge of the heart, hoping to add it to that knowledge currently recognized by the mind and aiming for the heart-vision eventually to assimilate that of the mind. However, even getting to the point of working on a view of the universe with others is also a matter of the heart, for it requires a tremendous amount of previous work building a foundation of love and respect.

Strictly speaking, we believe that the universe is one unitary thing. We also believe that it has a character, in that it seems to persist as itself. It has, in particular, been built on the elementary freedoms of spirit-matter. It has evolved in a self-consistent manner, showing continuity from the simplest of elements to complex organisms. Only this consistency has permitted us to describe it at all. Can we count on the persistence of the continuity of character? Will it possibly undergo a sudden change to a rationally explicable cosmos? From being a cosmos that sets problems by its very nature, might it suddenly become free of all future problems? A future free of problems is not one of the options inherent in this cosmos. I have been trying to show that life is only possible in a cosmos with the features we do indeed see. That is the Anthropic Principle. Then if these characteristics were deleted, life would be as impossible as it would have been from the start in such a cosmos.

A consistent universe does not suddenly change character, at least not in a fundamental attribute. Thus, if the newness-producing, or creative, quality of the universe is now the case, consistency seems to require that it will always be the case. It seems evident from the inherent contradictoriness of physical reality and the fact that it is always subject to interpretive adjustment of opposites that creativity is indeed a fundamental attribute. Is not this assertion also subject to interpretation? Yes, of course; that is the fun of being alive. But there are things that we know pretty well, such as the fact that the Earth is round and not flat. I am convinced that the contradictoriness of physical reality is on a par with the roundness of the Earth.

The same problem of integration arises in the action of "leading out" (see chapter 3) by which the cosmos attempts to enhance the individuality and creativity of persons and is ever interested to see what newness will emerge. Leading out encourages the uniqueness of the person, welcoming the expression of the true heart. It increases the diversity rather than the unity of the cosmos.

To be led out, one must somehow encounter two primary experiences, love and beauty, and it is clear from numerous cases that they can be experienced even by a child in a harsh parental environment, though there are perhaps limits. We experience love and beauty in many ways. Certainly, some are deeper and more fundamental than others. The ancient Greeks recognized this by having several terms for *love*, the most profound of which is what they called *agape*, the outgoing feeling of oneness with all of humanity and even with all of creation.[5]

Forgiveness, Love, and Freedom

Paul Tillich pointed out that it is impossible for one truly to love God while feeling rejected by God. He draws upon a scene from the life of Jesus for an illustration. A woman of the streets comes into a house where Jesus is at dinner with a Pharisee. Jesus perceives that the Pharisee is offended at her presence and by her actions toward Jesus (which show her feeling of having found forgiveness in her life) and gives a brief parable whose point is the concrete relationship of love and forgiveness: one to whom little is forgiven will not love much.[6] The Greek word for forgiveness, *aphesis*, means "release," setting free. To be unforgiven is to be imprisoned; to be forgiven is to be free, healed, mobile. If love desires the freedom of the other, then love releases, forgives.

I feel very deeply that the "heart of the universe" is love, experienced personally in the reality of freedom. It is experiencing freedom as being loved, being on the receiving end of the love relationship, being forgiven, liberated.

As Tillich points out, forgiveness always has the quality of something that occurs in spite of something else.[7] It is not that there is no such thing as hurting others but that there is indeed release in spite of the wounding. Not everyone comes easily to the acceptance of this aspect of reality. We often try to find release by saying that there was no wound, denying the hurt. By rationalizing in this manner, we prevent the actual release from the actual wound. The denial of the reality of the wound can actually induce us to take offense at our freedom and the fact that things are not set, so that we can just accept them. Instead, we must do our own exploring and, in that journey, discover the wound. *If we have not yet accepted the wound as a reality of the structure of the cosmos, it is bound to be interpreted as a flaw in the design.* But since freedom is inherent in things, it is the cosmos itself that leads us out, though this is not always, or even usually, a gentle process. Something presents us with a demand if we are chosen to become strong, creative individuals.

Creative individuality makes us all different. Yet we are all human and humanity can be recognized as one, in spite of its persistent divisions. Thus, the integration of a cosmos of individual sentient beings, each with an individual and unique "true heart," is a problem. How can even our little Earth contain both the unity and the diversity in one humanity, with all the problems that apparently divide us? Is there a "natural" process of integration that does not result in conformity? If there is, it clearly must be an unforced process, so that it is as inherent in evolved structures as any other fundamental attribute of a species, such as number of limbs, of eyes, fingers, ears, etc. Being led out is being led out of the bondage of unconsciousness into a liberated vantage point from which the person perceives and participates in the bondedness of the whole, which includes compassion and love.

Integration of Individuals

The cosmos is to be integrated in consciousness, wherever that occurs. We know that our own species is on the way to such an integrative consciousness, but the general trend of scientific knowledge indicates that the same developments are happening everywhere in visible space. Even here, so far, only a few individuals have achieved anything like a wholeness of humanity within themselves. They are the ones we revere as spiritual teachers, or as avatars of God, and who help move whole segments of humanity in a creative direction. Here, too, we might remember Jesus weeping over Jerusalem and ask what, in the ongoing state of our world, evokes the same response in ourselves. Thus, we still focus on the integration of the individual, for the sake of the planet.

The biological unity of an organism is not consciously maintained but amounts to an unconscious regulation of the totality. Jung discovered through analysis of psychological material that the psychological totality of human beings regulates itself in a similar manner. The psyche seeks in various ways to compensate partialities and expand the personality, and to push the individual across boundaries to new awarenesses. Seen from this perspective, all such processes have a unified goal, the wholeness and uniqueness of the individual. This center of functioning Jung called the Self. He described its activity as "the transcendent function," which engages us and alternates us back and forth between opposites, so that we can come to our own individual balance. The Self ensures that what is needed in our lives crosses our path, or rather that we are where we need to be in order to encounter what is needed. Since this occurs in the realm of meaning and thus is a matter of personal judgment, there is no scientific test of this reality but only the experience of countless individuals that it is so. One beautiful example is that of former United Nations Secretary-General Dag Hammarskjöld, as recorded in his book *Markings*:

> *I don't know Who—or what—put the question, I don't know when it was put. I don't even remember answering. But at some moment I did answer Yes to Someone—or Something—and from that hour I was certain that existence is meaningful and that, therefore my life, in self-surrender, had a goal.*[8]

Such awareness as he shows is indeed rare. "Integrative," as a quality of the cosmos, means that all of the fundamental qualities and aspects of the cosmos come together to form a web.

The wholeness or balance of the Self is not necessarily experienced by the individual, yet it manifests in individual lives and can be experienced. It is the interaction of the individual psyche with God, who is the ultimate complex of opposites, with whom "all things are possible."[9]

Irreversibility

That the process of integration, things coming together, the forming of bonds, makes energy available to the being has been a major theme of this book. Under the "prime law," all gatherings release energy. Part of that energy is always lost to the being, whether a star or a living organism. According to Ilya Prigogine, the expenditure or dissipation of this energy by an organism serves to concretize the individuality of that being because the loss is irreversible.[10]

An example of such an irreversible energy exchange on the human level is our having caused hurt to another human being or perhaps to an animal. I am thinking of those cases where we wish we could take back what we have done and find that we cannot: a permanent (irreversible) change has taken place. It could be physical, as in the case of an accident involving loss of an organ, a limb, or a life. It could involve the disclosure of an infidelity or a theft to support a gambling or drug habit. Such events can be strong determinants of our growing consciousness, as is witnessed in the common expression "sadder but wiser." The true process of personality formation leaves deep marks upon us, which become essential parts of our individuality. Life goes on.

In considering this, we might take time to meditate on what has most shaped our lives, including in that meditation events that we regarded as unmitigated disasters at the time, as well as those that gave us an unexpected lift.

It is the irreversible energy exchange processes that define individuality. The integration of the personality, the incorporation into its living of its potential wholeness and specificity, is achieved through the energy exchanges that constitute its life. The effect of personal history is indeed important. In terms of the psyche, the bond-forming energy that we expend involves not only persons but also ideas, images, and attitudes, whether intellectual, cultural, or religious.

The integration that brings consciousness is not a mental process but rather an empirical learning to encompass the great opposites such as intellect and emotion, not in concept but in feeling, that is, in life. Part of the difficulty lies in the fact that the achievement of consciousness involves the facing, owning, and integrating of the "shadow," which refers to all of our inner darknesses and unseen contradictions. That which we fear as unachievable, as too great for ourselves but which may nonetheless be a relentless demand upon us, is also part of our shadow. For us, it is dark, terrifying, even though it may be our maximum potential for strength and illumination.

Another difficulty lies in the fact that, of the forces that bring people and events together, some seem integrative in a positive sense, and some bring things to the test or even directly to a collision with a strong potential for mutual annihilation. This is the stuff of high drama, and we are fascinated by stories of such disastrous attractions, for their reality is also within ourselves. Some events come toward us with an inexplicable feeling of fate, holding out to us a truly unknown dimension. Perhaps it is so, but perhaps, as in *Romeo and Juliet*, it is a fateful entanglement, bringing together love and death. We are fascinated by the unknown.

We may ask ourselves whether a caring God would play such high-risk "games" with us, but inwardly we know that this way, in which we are free, is the only path to consciousness and integrity of being and that we may fail.[11] In fact, unless we find our own high-risk adventure, we will fail to find life. Life is worth something and therefore costs something. We can take offense at this cost. We often are deceived, often deceive ourselves, that life should be clear and easy.

That which brings about soul-shaping collisions must also be termed "integrative," and the meaning of this whole chapter must be seen with the understanding that integration has a dark, frightening side. The integrative aspect of the cosmos, which we know as the Self within humanity, brings together all things, none of which makes for an easy path to enlightenment. It is what we do with these collisions, how we respond, that makes all the difference for the meaning of our lives.

Persons grow and can achieve tremendous effect in the evolution and integration of the species. One of my favorite images of the physical cosmos is that it fits the ancient saying that God is a circle whose center is everywhere and whose circumference is nowhere. Jung's writings demonstrate that the same model fits the Self. In the physical cosmos, the most obvious symbol of this omnicenteredness lies in the fact that stars form everywhere, each of which responds to and becomes a gravitating center. As far as psychological integration is concerned, I consider those individuals who might be termed the bright stars of human love as the gravitating centers that demonstrate that the integration of the cosmos occurs in any place. I am deeply indebted to Erich Neumann once again, for coining the term *centroversion* to describe the operation of the Self in all humans. The Center of the universe is at work in each of us at every moment. As we integrate ourselves, with the help of the Self, with the whole cosmos (beginning with the whole Earth), we make it easier for the Self to do this work of centroversion, not only on Earth, I feel, but everywhere.

Though titled "Healing," the final chapter will be leading toward the idea of our being at home in our cosmos, even with all of its challenges. Certainly, the sense of healing is central to this possibility, as we assume the burden of finding and carrying our own wholeness, which means that we must undergo psychic death and rebirth countless times in our lives. The reward of this process is that we also grow in wisdom, consciousness, depth, and *lightness* of living. The Self, which lives in us and which we experience as our God-image, lies behind all life on all worlds. Our healing is grounded in the evolution of the whole cosmos; and, if we learn to participate in it, we participate in the healing of the whole.

CHAPTER 10

Healing

Clutch an hour of misrendered love,
pound floors with it.
Often that's the single action
with power enough
to put a band around pain,
bring blood to lungs.
. . . .
Love is
a center of no return.
It gives out hurt, healing,
glaciers, flames. Enter it.
You become a steward of vortex.
Bow to it. It is old,
has lawful ways. Hold on.
Pound floors but don't let go.

—SHEILA MOON, "Pound Floors"

The word *healing*, one of the most beautiful in English, is full of paradox, for it has no meaning apart from wounding and sickness. We want and need healing because we are part of a universe such as we have seen on our journey together through this book. Our experience is the experience of the cosmos itself; it is a world of opposites which cannot be held, which fall apart, a world of broken things, of unrealized intentions, of disease and loss.

It is also a world in which finite forms must be, and are, continually broken down and remade closer to the pattern of the cosmos. We die to make room for the next living forms, and our distant progeny will use our bodies' atoms in forms of living beyond our imagination.

It is the same in our own lives. We undergo psychic deaths many times during our physical lives, for the sake of a rebirth of energy in a more whole attitude toward life. In that sense, our present being is always a wound to the cosmos, to God, for it always could take on a form more apt to the hidden truth of reality. Saint Augustine said, "Love kills that which we were"; but this killing, although for the sake of something new, even for ourselves, is not a gentle thing. We will fear it as long as we have not learned to trust the renewal of life by forces and patterns much higher than ourselves. *The fullest form of healing is not the repair of what we have known, but a rebirth out of the death of something no longer serviceable to the Godding in us.* Thus, God in us is always the possibility of something beyond what we presently are. Peter rebuked Jesus for saying that what he was doing would lead to his death. Jesus called Peter's rebuke satanic, for Peter was bound up with human things, rather than considering what God needed from him.[1] This is the eternal battlefield, and yet these battles to sacrifice the lesser and embrace the greater values within ourselves will lead to healing and to fulfilled living.

In mortal combat, one antagonist dies, and there is an end to the battle. Immortal combat, the model for living in this cosmos, is more like the poem in the epigraph. If we can hold on, we can experience the meaning of things at a new level of depth, and this experience is one of profound healing, of at-one-ness with the universe. Our psyche is restructured in the process. The antagonists, the great opposites of life, go on living and learning, gaining in both strength and love, for they gain in the realization that they are building a world which is becoming conscious of its own meaning. I speak purposely of the opposites as living beings, for, as we work with them, they do develop. And we develop as well, in struggling with their struggles in us. Thus, an aspect of healing is learning to accept the world as it is and to live joyfully in it in spite of its darkness and pain.

Wholeness and Healing

Everything that is, from atoms to living beings, has a specific wholeness pattern of its own. More complex beings, such as humans, have not only a physical (spirit-matter) wholeness pattern (human physiology) and a human psychic wholeness pattern but an *individual potential meaning* to their lives, a specific complex of opposites that must be integrated into living in order to fulfill destiny. As that pattern is distorted, most commonly by evading some of the needed opposites, the being experiences disease, even if the disorder is not felt as such. This is a common result of the unconscious and partial way in which most of us live. I would trust, however, that no one who is reading this is in that state of being comfortable with partial living, of having finally sacrificed a desire for something greater from life. Our wholeness pattern, our individual path to completion as human beings, calls us ever to return to the journey.

Our work on our own wholeness and healing is part of healing the earth and ultimately of healing the cosmos, by which I mean the fulfillment of the meaning of life for each moment it endures. No being can ever comprehend its ultimate meaning, but, at any given moment, life can be lived to a maximum. Taking the suffering that leads to wholeness upon ourselves is symbolically the same as bringing to actuality the Christ-center within ourselves. It also fulfills the quite independent motif of the "suffering servant" of Isaiah, "with whose stripes we are healed."[2]

To take this a step further, here is a passage from Jung to which I return again and again in seeking courage for living:

> *We rightly associate the idea of suffering with a state in which the opposites violently collide with one another, but we hesitate to describe such a painful experience as being "redeemed." Yet it cannot be denied that the great symbol of the Christian faith, the Cross, upon which hangs the suffering figure of the Redeemer, has been emphatically held up before the eyes of Christians for nearly two thousand years. . . . All opposites are of God, therefore we must bend to this burden; and in so doing we find that God's "oppositeness" has taken possession of us, has become incarnated in us. We become vessels filled with divine conflict.*[3]

This makes it abundantly clear that achieving wholeness is far from easy.

We know well enough from physics that opposites are present in every so-called particle in the cosmos, but Jung's statement attributes "all opposites" to God. Indeed, our various images and attributes given to God contain qualities and their opposites, such as same/other, present/distant, personal/universal, masculine/feminine, loving/wrathful, forgiving/jealous, and so many more. But if God already has all opposites perfectly united, why is it our task to take them upon ourselves? If our life has a purpose, there must be a task that is both essential to the universe—to God—*and capable of fulfillment only by finite beings.* There is a healing task for us, which is no less than to complete the cosmos through our own being.

Healing is not, of course, something that we can do simply by thinking about it, gathering equipment, and pushing through. We need the help of the cosmos, of God; and we still cannot do it unless we ourselves are willing to be healed in turn, with all that it costs to undertake that process. We must put aside our ego-bound intentions, our egocentric will, and permit the universe to heal itself in us, by putting ourselves at its service without reservation. That is no small requirement.

The task of living so as to manifest a healing in a piece of the cosmos, the task that only we can do for God, is ours because of the nature of psyche, compounded, as it is, of spirit and matter. The primordial cosmos is pure spirit-matter, undifferentiated by any perceiving being. Only psyche is capable of contrast-knowing; thus only psyche can serve the self-awareness of God.

We who have that self-reflexivity can use it to serve ourselves or become instruments of the Divine.

To receive the messages that we need in that process, we must reorient ourselves to listen within, to listen to that of the field that is moving in us. Animals, and humans who have not developed their contrast-knowledge strongly, can listen to the field with considerably greater ease than those who have developed it, but their knowing of the larger needs of the cosmos is more limited, as is their field of action. All who listen to the field find the messages they receive from it are appropriate to their lives. The true mystic, though, is one who both possesses a strongly developed contrast-knowing and has given over the use of her or his being to the greater need of the cosmos. The specific ability of the more fully developed mind is the understanding of the nature of the cosmos by means of contrast-knowledge.[4] It gives us a knowledge of God that can come by no other means.

Psyche and Cosmos

Psyche concentrates as an individual develops, just as a star forms in response to the centering pull of gravity on the matter in a galaxy. Centroversion, described in the previous chapter, is the equivalent of psychic gravity, which attracts psychic contents. I pointed out that gravity has an analogy to love but also that it is but one of four forces at work in the physical cosmos. By analogy, centroversion would be only one of several psychic counterparts to the physical forces. Gravity is the weakest but most pervasive of the physical forces; and the analogous statement, that centroversion is the most subtle but most pervasive of the psychic forces, seems an apt spiritual comparison.

Psyche becomes consolidated in individual beings out of the weaving of opposites in the lives of those beings. For instance, in our recent history, we have strongly differentiated physical things from spiritual things, to the point that we have felt an insoluble conflict between science and religion, at least if we have considered the matter at all fully. How can spirit and matter, religion and science, heart and mind, be reunited in our lives? It is a great work to honor both fully and yet integrate them fully in our daily lives without flinching from any fact in either dimension. That weaving is not easy.

As we undertake the weaving of heart and mind, however, the psyche proceeds to build or accumulate in the cosmos as the sum of the *lived* wholeness patterns of individual beings. The patterns overlap and interact. Our "within" is connected to the within of others, and as we live in freedom, the benefits are mutual to all.

There is evidence that psychic contents which might come to consciousness but which have not done so are stored throughout our bodies, so that listening to our bodies is a source of clues as to what is needed in our lives. We are holograms of the living cosmos. Each of us has a unique piece to work with, but only by including all humanity (with its deadly religious conflicts) and even all of life can we get even a glimpse of a more whole world.

The process of meditation reveals much to us of that patterned energy flow, but who can say how much? It is a continual process:

we become aware of it only when we attend to it. There is much more available than we have yet discovered, no matter who we are. Nor will we discover all of it through meditation alone. We also need interpersonal interaction, in order to learn to be ourselves in fullness, as well as to be integral with the cosmos.

The wholeness pattern of the universe is present everywhere and at all times, in the field of our immediate spiritual surroundings. The form that the wholeness image of the cosmos takes in individual beings is the wholeness image of our own psyches, containing all that we need for the completion of our own finite lives and the fulfillment of our piece of the whole.

Every integration of something real of the universe is a kind of healing of the image of the cosmos, even the image of God, within ourselves. Thus far, we are not very complete images of the macrocosm; we have many distorted images of the cosmos and of God as well. This is the way it is, and the only way it could be; for an endless time would be needed, along with an infinite openness to revision of our understanding, for the wholeness of the universe to be completed in us. It is not for any finite being to experience.

Our finite consciousness, however, with all its true and distorted vision of the cosmos and of God, is all that is available for God's self-realization. Where we feel and act upon our sense of God's desire for love, justice, and knowing, then, in that unique situation, God acts through us and realizes the meaning of it in our consciousness.

This would apply to all sentient creatures and their experiences, however strange they might seem to us, throughout the universe.

Psyche is in-between spirit and matter, woven of both and separate from the ultimate nature of both. We too are in-between, and only from that middleness can the opposites be seen.

This suggests that somehow the glue that holds the cosmos together, in the sense of giving it unity consciously, so that it becomes the self-aware cosmos, is the accumulated psyche that we have been considering. Only where psyche has arisen does the cosmos become *the* cosmos, and only then can it become *home* for living beings. Prior to that, there was no such question.

The fact that the opposites can meet in the psyche, though the rational faculty would hold them apart, is the source of a great deal of human longing for some kind of absolute knowing and connection or a sense of safe haven. Paradoxically, it is the ego that is disconnected and feels lost when it carries the contrast-function to extremes. In chapter 3, I quoted physicist Steven Weinberg's view that the more the universe is comprehensible, the more it seems pointless. This is an example of the lostness that results from too much reliance on contrast-knowledge. The profundity of human loneliness has inspired much poetry and philosophy. Where we feel solidly grounded, it is from the side of the field alone, not from what the ego knows. That is, the knowing ego must not refuse to acknowledge the support of the field. Erich Neumann puts it rather well:

> *Even if to all appearances our normal life exists exclusively within the world of the opposites, the world of subject and object, in fact this only happens when we are completely identified with the ego, the center of our conscious minds. The case is different, however, if we are living as "whole persons," beyond the range of ego-centered existence.*[5]

Neumann says that it is impossible for us to maintain a complete identification with our egos permanently; the cause, he says, is "centroversion, which represents the tendency of our totality to realize itself."[6] However, we often can and do refuse to recognize that which takes us beyond our egos, even to get us through a given day, which we certainly could not do on the attention of our egos alone.

Changes in the psyche and its attitudes, which might permit our deeper healing, are beset with the greatest difficulties: merely seeing other possible ways of doing things does not automatically bring the individual to a choice of ways on the basis of interior values. Usually the individual exhibits a great stability of preference for those ways that were inculcated in childhood, and because of this structural stability, a person does not engage in free choice but rather chooses for the known collective values.

We always begin our inquiry from within the psyche, and in the end, the psyche is the integrating factor of the cosmos. Thus, the cosmos brings forth a *healing from within*. It is a process that begins in a small way, on the surfaces of planets where life concentrates and complexifies.

The self-realization, or consciousness, which the cosmos needs for its completeness was not present in the early cosmos. This is not to say that the cosmos is now complete, for our present consciousness clearly is of the most elementary sort, when judged by the general moral development of humanity. In principle there is no limit to the creative possibilities for consciousness in the cosmos. The cosmos is incomplete *in its very essence* and must, therefore, evolve indefinitely, ever increasing in consciousness, freedom, and love, in the ever deeper realization of its own meaning.

Psychic Energy and Symbols

Consciousness and freedom are both attributes of finite beings, and both require energy. The presence and availability of energy has been another major theme in our examination of the re-envisioning of the cosmos, at those points where we encountered the "prime law of physics," the release of energy in the gathering of matter or psyche. We build consciousness as we permit centroversion to retrieve the pieces of the cosmos and incorporate them into the life of the finite psyche. The energy released in the process accumulates as the light of knowing and the ability to influence the assimilation of the same contents by others.

But the energy of the cosmos does not just carry us along. Our own will and work are required.

For something to become conscious, two conditions must be met. There must be an organic carrier of sufficient complexity to carry the consciousness, and that carrier must be able to develop energy in excess of bare subsistence needs. That is, some of that energy comes from the physical side of things, from the health of our bodies. Some of the energy, however, seems to accumulate within, as we develop our minds and wisdom. The energy issue is two-sided. Not only must the carrier have the energy to devote to this new development, but the contents that are to come to consciousness must gain sufficient energy to get our attention. It is a common experience that some things, such as attractions to specific persons, things, or ideas, are so strong that we cannot avoid giving attention to them. We are obsessed by them. Others, when we do become aware of them, seem to have been around for some time in a fainter form but did not earlier have enough energy to break into our awareness. In general, an emergent content must have symbolic value to come to consciousness.

Symbols serve a major function in gathering energy to an inner area that will later come to consciousness. They first attract our devotion. We have all felt the fascination with some symbol that drew us to give attention or energy to it, until the meaning that drew us toward it in the first place became insight, that is, was then added to our awareness. From there, it can become part of our consciousness if we can use its energy to make it a part of our way of living. It is at this third step that we most often fail to build our insights into our lives, for to do so generally requires a change of attitude and a struggle with parts of ourselves that have long assumed that the world was as we formerly thought it to be. Otherwise, we do not really participate in the healing.

It is clear that a person cannot be free without sufficient energy, that energy increases freedom, but only if there is sufficient consciousness to harness the energy to some use, as in the image of "work" discussed in chapter 8. Just as a horse must be "broken" in order to become a companion in freedom, psychic energy must be tamed. At this point, consciousness begins to work against unbridled energy and undertakes the *opus contra naturam,* the work contrary to nature, for pure nature is untrammeled flow. In this way, consciousness, a product of nature, undertakes the *completing* of nature as a *work* to do, entering into the total process with freedom and will.

Here, too, symbols play an essential, if sometimes dangerous, role. The appearance of someone who affirms a new direction for humanity has a very powerful effect on others.

Buddha, Confucius, Jesus, and the other revered religious innovators provided such symbols for many, galvanizing their psyches to action and sacrifice. The remarkable *creative will* exercised by such innovators emphasizes the relationship of their new visions of reality to the release of energy in their activity. Energy also gets dammed up in a whole culture, but the average person cannot draw upon that energy, or cross that boundary, until a bridge is formed by the symbols brought by the creative individual.[7] In other words, one might say that energy had been built up in humanity at the time of Jesus so that people were "ready for him," as a creative individual, to help in the release of that energy and in the partial healing of the world that followed.

With all of the suffering that has followed the creative innovators, in the form of religious wars, one might be justified in saying that it would have been better had they never appeared. But I do not think any of us would rather that such were the case because of the benefits we have derived from our religions. The whole picture shows the pain of transformation on a large scale, but the same wars go on within each of us, if we are called to transformation as individuals.

Consciousness, in the form of God-awareness, is the ultimate product of the cosmos and the emblem of integration. It is integrated into life via the moral dimension alone. Otherwise, the face of God is not integrated into our own true faces. *The integration of the face of God into the cosmos, through our faces, is the re-envisioning of the cosmos with the heart.*

In finding the place of the spirit in the cosmos as a whole, we have been building a fuller picture of reality. In one sense, we have merely added the things of the heart, life, and spirituality to those of the mind; but in a deeper sense, the whole picture has changed. As I have often said in the course of this book, after we have done our re-envisioning, our view of the cosmos begins with the oneness, the wholeness of the cosmos. Never again can we be satisfied with a partial vision such as the view of the intellect alone, the purely "scientific" view, whoever we are and whatever we do.

Are We Home?

We live *here,* or we fail to live. Whether we are bound or free does not depend on whether we stay on Earth or travel to the stars. Having a comfortable life is likewise irrelevant. Living with evolving meaning depends on being open to what is and taking it inside, in the sense both of truly seeing and of living in accord with reality. If our door is open, open to strangers, to the strange, as in the ancient traditions of hospitality, then we are home. If we can be open and yet be such that nothing can threaten us, we are home.

Our world, our cosmos, is full of pain. Does that push us away or draw us in? That is perhaps the central question that will answer for us the question of whether we are home. In a sense that we all recognize in times of disaster, pain is the web of humanity, for it draws us together and draws forth our greatly unused ability to love. If our experience of pain, whether our own pain or of that of others, teaches us to love and to risk ourselves, rather than to avoid love and risk, then we have entered it as home.

Our world, our cosmos, our universe, has a nature that is at one with itself throughout. That includes its nonrational roots, the basis of both freedom and life; and it includes life itself in its physical finitude; and it includes the inevitability of conflict. It has been said that maturity is the ability to live with conflict, which assuredly applies to whole peoples as much as it does to individuals. If we can handle freedom and if we can learn to handle conflict, again we can be said to be home.

Our world, or any world in our cosmos, is a world of beauty, showing forth the infinite, even in a square foot of desert ground. If we take it as an offering of a look at something magnificent and as an opportunity to love and be loved, to drink the mutual cup of the heart together and to savor the food of the mind as well, then, whether we live on the road or in a palace, we are at home.

We find home when we take our place in the world as it is, with all its gifts, with all its sorrows. The cosmos sets for us problems that only love can solve. Until we see that love can solve them, we are blind, whether blinded by our egocentric wants or by some rationalistic view of reality. By now you know that, by love, I do not mean something sweet. Rather I mean our openness, presence, and work at healing the wounds we find, wherever we are.

Is *God* at home in our world? If *we* are at home here, the answer is "Yes!"

APPENDIX I

Contrast-Knowledge and Field-Knowledge

We "know" in various ways. All of my own studies have been guided by the idea that science and religion are two ways of knowing that complement each other. Only such an attitude can show forth what is common to all humanity, as divided as it feels on issues of science versus religion. Complementarity, a concept developed by Neils Bohr to account for certain phenomena encountered in physics, is the recognition that logically contradictory concepts must be employed in providing a complete description of elementary (microphysical) particles and fields. All of the "building blocks" of physical being are "third points"; that is, each is an ultimate unity of opposites.

In our attempts to come to a rational understanding of nature, we have developed the process of forming these logical contrasts, but now we discover that they do not apply in an ultimate sense. Our understanding of physical reality has reached a level of sophistication at which we can begin to see the ultimate unity begin to reassert itself.

To state the obvious, all progress of knowledge consists of differentiating what previously was undifferentiated. At the same time, humans universally feel an attraction to what might be known but is at present only intuited; or instead of active attraction, some only have the vague feeling that "something else is there." Physicist Michael Polanyi describes this state in his book *Personal Knowledge*:

> *All mental unease that seeks appeasement of itself will be regarded as a line of force in a morphogenetic field. Just as mechanical forces are the gradients of a potential energy, so this field of forces would also be the gradient of a potentiality; a gradient arising from the proximity of a possible achievement. Our sense of approaching the unknown solution to a problem, and the urge to pursue it, are manifestly responses to a gradient of potential achievement.*[1]

This statement gives a good sense of what Neumann calls "field-knowledge." It also provides a nice model for the subjective, or faith, element in the winning of contrast-knowledge.

Contrast-Knowledge

In the usual idealized image of science, a proof does not simply confirm that the results of experiment agree with the corresponding theory concerning a phenomenon in question but must go an additional step. It must also account for and exclude all possible causes of a phenomenon except one, or one irreducible set of causes. Reduction is the ultimate isolation of "variables" and the contrast of the observed state of affairs and its immediate causes with all of the surrounding flux. In this view, the idea of "order out of chaos" is the winning of a bit of contrast-knowledge from the chaotic background. For Ilya Prigogine, whose best-known book is in fact titled *Order out of Chaos*, it is entirely different.[2] He points us toward chaos as the locus of a new, more subtle, wider-reaching order. Prigogine's work shows a profound link between our growing contrast-knowledge and the field from which that knowledge is precipitated.

We also commonly say that we see by contrast of "figure" and "ground." What we usually call seeing truly is a contrast phenomenon: it is forming an image, by means of which the thing seen stands out, is isolated. That which is accessible to our ego-consciousness is contrast.

Contrast includes the contrast of ego and world: that which we call "becoming" in the case of a person, which makes visible the qualities of the individual.

In *The Place of Creation,* psychologist Erich Neumann said:

> *The world of our modern conscious minds is the world of rationality and of discrimination: its instrument is the separation of pairs of opposites. . . . [The viewpoint] of our conscious minds and of our culture, conditioned as it is by the patriarchal outlook, is based on a principle of radical separation, carried through to the point of actual splitting, between the conscious mind and the unconscious, the psyche and the world, the ego and the Self, "reality" and the unitary reality. The disintegration of the world into dead and unrelated sections, which we observe in psychosis, is only a caricature of our own existence.*[3]

One need hardly remark that science has largely succeeded, to date, in accomplishing the same sectioning into dead elements.

By means of contrast, of figure-ground relationships, we form images. This done, we begin to sort out similarities and differences to classify. Our perception of contrast becomes more subtle but keeps its primary character as contrast.

When, as is inevitable, we ourselves become the focus of our learning, our drive to form contrasts works to cut us loose from the very world itself. This separation from the world we then call "objectivity," even "scientific" objectivity.

Field-Knowledge

We have been living under the domination of a one-sided patriarchal worldview, which actually seeks to "liberate" itself from its undeniable, nonrational roots. That is the ultimate goal of rationalism. If we attempt to recognize those roots, we must conclude that our contrast-knowledge is just one kind of knowledge out of perhaps several. But that which does not show contrast—what is that? Is it even a "that?" Neumann calls it "field-knowledge." As soon as we see that possibility, we begin to explain a whole segment of human experience, including our encounter with the Divine, and what philosopher Martin Heidegger called *dasein:* "being there," at the border-region of emergence, where concepts are not operative but where a fundamental aliveness prevails. What lies beyond that border, Neumann calls the "unitary reality." Jung and von Franz call it by the ancient name *unus mundus*, the one-world, or the world of one-ness.

If we reflect upon how we come to know something in a clear manner, we must make room for all those living experiences that give us a feeling of "approach" to something important, which Polanyi described so beautifully above. In the same part of *Personal Knowledge*, he says:

> *Recall the process of scientific discovery. This process is not specifiable in terms of strict rules, for it involves a modification of the existing interpretive framework. It crosses a gap and causes thereby a self-modification of the intelligence achieving the discovery. In the absence of any formal procedure on which the discoverer could rely, he/she is guided by his/her intimations*

> *of a hidden knowledge. She/he senses the proximity of something unknown and strives passionately towards it.*[4]

Since the discovery is real, that is, it is a discovery of the nature of something as it already was before the discovery was made, Polanyi insists that the researcher, though initially lacking the contrast with which to see it in contrast-knowledge, truly senses it nonetheless.

Another helpful definition of a kind of field-knowledge, by W. H. Auden, is "all that we know, so long as no one asks."[5]

I have found the diagram in figure App. 1 useful:

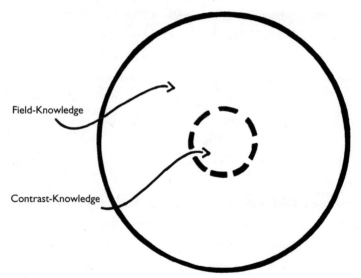

FIGURE APP. 1 Field-knowledge vs. contrast-knowledge

The inner circle is dotted, in recognition that it is permeable to the sort of not-quite-yet-knowledge experiences just described. The main point, however, is that what we have gained in the circle of contrast-knowledge is just a tiny part of what is available and present to us at all times, even if we are unconscious of it. As Neumann says:

APPENDIX I

> *We have perceived that the archetypes are elements of the unitary reality. But they are also invariably umbilical points of contact with it, as it were, since wherever the archetypal world forces its way into our life and exerts a determining influence upon it, we are—even if we do not know it—in touch with the unitary reality.*[6]

That is, though we can, under favorable conditions, recognize that there are archetypal behaviors and influences, we tend to forget their existence when thinking of what we know. We do so because we usually find their influences disturbing when we think about them. If we have an archetypal anger, or loss of "composure," we typically want to forget about it! We want to be "self-sufficient" in our contrast-world.

> *However, this attempt to live as nothing but an ego in a nothing-but-polar world of the conscious mind is rendered impossible by the psychological fact that for better or for worse we are expelled from this one-sidedness by our own totality and by the indwelling, dynamic process of centroversion which represents the tendency of this totality to realize itself.*[7]

To our usual "conscious" prejudice, this is a remarkable statement. It asserts not merely that seeing our archetypes with an open mind would force us to recognize their reality but that the process Neumann terms "centroversion" is at work in each of us, compelling us to become conscious of the "totality" of being so that the unitary reality may "realize itself." We are drawn to the Center, which is the heart of our human religious longing.

This is a persistent human experience and one that engenders conflicts with our desire for scientific knowledge and objectivity. One might even say that, since the emergence of the ego is an activity of the Self, the fact that the ego also fights against

APPENDIX I

acknowledgment of the totality means that the Center is fighting against its own emergence. Nevertheless, the whole process shows that the self-consciousness of the unitary reality progresses as we are forced more and more to acknowledge that reality.

APPENDIX 2

The Cycle of Archaic Identity

The Evolution of Consciousness in the Collective

Even in our own times, when we come to a new scientific understanding, we tend to assume that our new knowledge now lets us see how things *really* are, and we seem not to have learned that this process will continue cyclically into the unknown future. To the extent that we fall prey to this error, we actually reestablish the archaic identity of subject and object because we imagine that things really are what we imagine them to be. We thereby regress to the state of the infant in which there is no distinction of subject and object. Of course, this is a partial regression, but it shows up a gap in our understanding of the fundamental nature of things, which is that our knowledge can never be complete, for we do not know, and cannot know, things as they are in themselves.

The pieces of our knowledge of ourselves and of the world that are filled in with each cycle of projected assumptions and painful

APPENDIX 2

learning are the building blocks of our ultimate personality, that is, what we are able to achieve of our self-actualization in this life.

In the end, we may be able to realize consciously the fact that we are indeed one with the universe at our roots and shape our lives to live from this fact. In a sense, the archaic identity of subject and object is the ultimate truth; we are part of this universe, and the universe is one. Although the experience of this unity is called the "beatific vision," we cannot live our earthly lives in that experience; we must deal with the "ten thousand things," the "nitty-gritty" of existence. On the other hand, we cannot escape the ultimate truth.

1. *Archaic Identity: The world is alive with gods, or with divine power.* All external events are divine actions. The individual feels called/driven/not responsible.   Animism

2. *First separation: natural law, inertial world.* There is a tendency to see God as a World Principle, more distant, more universal, less personal. Astronomical eclipses and conjunctions are seen as predictable. Emergence is bifurcation into opposites.   Gods/World

3. *Moral obstacles to separation/nonseparation.* On the one hand, humans begin to permit themselves moral judgments of "gods," and, on the other, they assert the incomprehensibility of God's wisdom on moral grounds.   God's World

4. *Denial of external soul/mystery.* Thinkers begin to assert that the divine is a projection. There is also a self-assertion of human   Enlightenment

consciousness (humanism) and an apotropaic need for explanation. The reaction to this is a retreat into symbolism: pushing the divine further away but reserving a special world that communicates with ours symbolically. The creation story becomes an allegory of the rise of human souls. *This stage holds the danger of rationalistic devaluations, unless the elder religious images can be given some work to do.* (Part of my own work lies in this area of keeping the spirit present in science, tied to the phenomena.)

5. *Reflection.* The inner source is acknowledged; the outer phenomena are reinterpreted. There is always more of the cosmos to see and assimilate. Insofar as a new discovery is seen as a final truth, stage 1 is reasserted. Insofar as something is taken inside, there is an increase of consciousness; we have greater stability and control of events. *We have more freedom, choices, and responsibility.*

          Seeing

Notes

The epigraphs at the front of the book are from Neumann 1989, 5; and Saint-Exupéry 1943, 87.

PREFACE
1. Emanuel Swedenborg, 1996, §27.
2. Kierkegaard 1962, 32–34.

PROLOGUE: LOVING
The epigraph is from Auden 1976, 221–222.
1. Williams 1949, 68.
2. Following a suggestion by my wife Carrie, I use the word *feeling* as the primordial root of both emotions and intellect, and as the goal of their reunification. Our emotions are often ungrounded in true feeling and are like wild, lost animals. Where the depth is present with emotion, we have feeling, but the same is true where depth is present with intellect.
3. Reps n.d., 75.
4. One of the playful aspects of writing is to discover that the paragraphs do not end up in the same order as they were written. This is part of what says to me that the writer is not my ego, but something else within me. But I must also participate, to discover, again through play, the needed order of the material.
5. Neumann 1989, 216–217.
6. Lusseyran 1987, 281.
7. Ibid., 300.

8. Patchen 1969, 359.
9. Werfel 1942.
10. Werfel 1976.
11. Johnson 1937, 77.

CHAPTER 1: EVOLVING
The epigraphs are from Rumi 1990, 41; and Jung 1963, 348. The quotation from Rumi is printed by permission of its translator, Coleman Barks.
1. Matthew 11:15; 13:9, 43; Mark 4:9, 23; Luke 8:8, 14:35.
2. Jung 1963, 103–104.
3. In many stars, there is a different source of pressure as well, but we can neglect that source for the sake of our analogy.
4. See Prigogine and Stengers 1986, 175 specifically; and, in general, throughout the work.
5. Our body temperature of 98.6°F., or 37°C., can also be given as an "absolute" temperature of 310 Kelvins. The cosmic background radiation has a temperature of 2.7 Kelvins, so that, in absolute terms, we are over a hundred times as hot as the universe. Incidentally, the human body temperature falls at a point on the temperature scale that divides the temperature range between the freezing and boiling points of water roughly in a "Golden Section." (The exact golden mean occurs at 38.1°C., rather than our 37.1°C.)
6. Weinberg 1979; Hawking 1988.

7. Teilhard de Chardin 1969, 23.
8. I have gone into the Patterning at length in Hitchcock 1986 and Hitchcock 1991.
9. Quoted in Verdet 1984, 24.
10. It certainly seems possible that the unrealized options might remain somehow viable in the unconscious "field" (see just below in the text) and influence future choices. Yet the path taken is the path taken, and the other was not taken.
11. My own dissertation, "A Comparison of 'Complementarity' in Quantum Physics with Analogous Structures in Kierkegaard's Philosophical Writings, from a Jungian Point of View" (Hitchcock 1976), showed this transphysics application in detail. I have also dealt with it in my other books (Hitchcock 1986 and Hitchcock 1991).
12. The "negative" energy is the gravitational relationship of all of the parts of the cosmos, while the "positive" energy is manifested in the radiation and matter of the cosmos, as well as its internal motions. In 1961, Marcel Golay suggested that the total energy of the cosmos is zero, which is the first such suggestion of which I know (Golay 1961). In *A Brief History of Time*, Stephen Hawking (1988, 129) says the same thing, without attribution to an earlier source.
13. I have placed a fairly full discussion of field-knowledge and contrast-knowledge in appendix 1.
14. Jung 1969b, par. 579.
15. In *Projection and Recollection in Jungian Psychology*, Marie-Louise von Franz (1980a, 179–199 [chapter 9]) has dealt

very creatively with the physics of reflection and its psychic parallels. The idea is that psychic energy is reflected in a manner analogous to that of light or other forms of electromagnetic energy being reflected by metals (electrical conductors).

The ego and the Self are mutual reflectors, as are the psyche and the objective world of spirit-matter. These two pairs of reflectors form a fourfold system that she pictures as shown below:

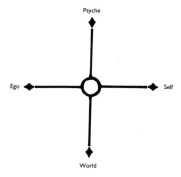

The ego is reflected by the Self in dreams, where we are often pictured in a way that compensates our conscious attitude and self-image, while the Self and its meaning are reflected to the ego by means of "synchronistic" events: those seemingly chance happenings that convey meaning to the ego. That is, the ego *sees* a meaning, or the event is not synchronistic. The Self thus guides us to a meaning. The world is reflected in the psyche as our world-image of something external to ourselves, and the psyche is reflected in the world by means of the mechanism of projection.

16. I have discussed this dynamic at some length in another book (Hitchcock 1991), but will give a brief summary in a later chapter, "Godding."
17. Neumann 1989, 8. Again, I have placed a fuller discussion in appendix 1.
18. It would not be particularly new to suggest that creation was a moral conflict for God, for others have remarked that, even if God were not responsible for evil, the arising of evil must have at least been foreseen in the divine consciousness. Either way, it "reflects" unfavorably upon the divine morality from a human point of view.
19. Boehme 1965, 1–12.
20. Jung 1969b, pars. 385–402.
21. Jung 1969b, pars. 579–583.
22. Hitchcock 1991.
23. Tillich 1948, 153–163, and Tillich 1952.
24. Tillich 1952, 164.
25. I have discussed the "within" in *The Web of the Universe* (Hitchcock 1991). However, since I wrote that book, a new phenomenon has been discovered that provides apt symbolism. The phenomenon is the existence of carbon forms known as Buckminster Fullerenes, or buckyballs, for short. If you can picture a hollow sphere made of sixty smaller spheres, you have the idea. Each smaller sphere, representing a single carbon atom, is bonded to those spheres that are next to it on the surface of the larger sphere, but there are no bonds between atoms across the hollow interior. This is the nature of the first buckyball to be predicted and discovered. Now, however, other forms are being discovered, which have bonds across the interior as well as along the surface. This additional structure gives new overall forms, increasing the complexity and potentials of the Fullerenes, as well as giving a visualization of an internal structure, or "within," which can be complexified in our imaginations as an internal web of being in living organisms.
26. Neumann 1989, 24–25.

CHAPTER 2: SELF-CREATING
The epigraph is from Hirschfield 1994, 139.

1. In terms of the field-knowledge/contrast-knowledge distinction that is made in chapter 8, we might say that the electron or photon always brings the field along with it, whichever of its two contradictory characteristics it is displaying at the moment.
2. In this book, I will keep the discussion as simple as possible by referring to photons as the example of an entity that exhibits this behavior, although other particles do so also. In fact, all physical objects can be said to exist in wave form, a condition discussed below in the text.
3. The intellect/emotion pair is not the same as the rational/nonrational pair. Charles Williams (1958, 102) used the term *the feeling intellect* to indicate something similar. Our contrast-knowledge is rational, as far as it goes, and field-knowledge is nonrational, as will be discussed below.
4. Teilhard de Chardin 1969, 23.

NOTES

5. Hitchcock 1986
6. If an atom were a *single* particle, it could not contain energy. Because the nucleus and the electron or electrons associated with that nucleus can change their relationships or arrangements, they can contain varying amounts of energy.
7. The source of the image is White 1931, 1423. The figure is a picture of a mechanical model and not a direct photo of an atom. The model is designed to exhibit the solution to a mathematical equation (Schrödinger's equation), which describes matter quite generally but which can be solved fully only in the case of hydrogen.
8. See for example Weisskopf 1979, 137. For a much fuller account, see Hitchcock 1991, 25–48 (chapter 1, "What is Spirituality?").
9. Teilhard de Chardin 1959, 41; 45. The published title of this book is *The Phenomenon of Man*, which, in suggesting to modern ears some restriction to the male human, is not only out of date but untrue to the French.
10. This point is stressed by Weisskopf 1979, 137.
11. Kuhn 1970, 52.
12. Einstein 1954, 28.
13. Murry 1930, 182–183.
14. Ibid., 182–183.
15. Ibid., 182–183.
16. Kierkegaard 1948, 104
17. Howes, in conversation with the author, Middletown, Conn., 1975.

CHAPTER 3: UNFOLDING BEAUTY
The epigraph is from Dickinson 1960, 412.
1. Buber 1947, 251.

2. This is the subjective side of the values discussed in the previous chapter. What I experience as meaning, an observer will identify as what I value.
3. Otto 1958, 12–30.
4. Weinberg 1979, 144.
5. Dyson 1979, 251. See the beginning of chapter 4 below.
6. Main and Seng 1965, 140.
7. Ibid., 140.
8. *Julius Caesar*, 1.2.191.
9. Jung 1971, par. 357.
10. Jung 1975, 139.
11. Blake 1975, plate 10.
12. Kazantzakis 1966, 284–285.
13. van der Leeuw 1963, 104–105.
14. John 10:30 and Revelation 21:5.
15. "For the Time Being: A Christmas Oratorio" in Auden 1965, 138.

CHAPTER 4: GODDING
The epigraph from Origen is quoted in Jung 1968, par. 624. Jung in turn cites the original source as *Leviticum Homiliae*, 5, 2, in *Patrologiae Completus*, vol. 12 of the Greek Series, edited by Jacques Paul Migne (Paris, 1857–1866), col. 449.
1. In chapters 7 and 8, I will address the question of whether our distinction of inner and outer has an ultimate validity. It is our ego-consciousness that is convinced, on "good evidence," that the distinction is quite clearly true in a sense so absolute as to be unquestionable. Certain phenomena, especially the dynamics of psychological projection and the ending of projections, lead us to question not only the inner/outer distinction but the exclusive use of the term *knowledge* for the

NOTES

other kind of knowing that are not the contrast-knowledge of ego-consciousness.
2. Dyson 1979, 252.
3. In *Cosmos*, Carl Sagan (1980, 269–289) has written a beautiful chapter about this called "The Persistence of Memory." Using examples from the songs of whales to the library of ancient Alexandria, he gives an impressive accounting of the information needs of a species that desires to take the whole cosmos into account.
4. This mode of expression is only the way in which our ego-consciousness attempts to express the presence of the field and the fact that the opposites are derived from the Patterning of the field. Therefore, it is an awkward rational expression for what Zen, Buddhism terms "thusness."
5. See my discussion of involution in Hitchcock 1991, 186–197, and Hitchcock 1999, 133–137.
6. Jung 1971, par. 700.
7. Definitions can indeed be made precise in the abstract, but each concrete object defies the definition in some respect, or if the definition is revised, e.g., from "is red" to "has some red impression in it," the definition loses sharpness.
8. We *represent* opposites by separating them, for example, into "figure" and "ground."
9. Otto 1958.
10. See appendix 1 for further discussion of contrast-knowledge and field-knowledge.
11. von Franz 1980a, 157.
12. Mollenkott 1987, 1–3; quoting Blake 1969, 117 ("The Divine Image" in *Songs of Innocence*).
13. Ibid., 65.
14. Ibid., 11.
15. Mark 14:36.
16. Mark 12:41–44.
17. In "Transformation Symbolism in the Mass" (Jung 1969b, pars. 385–402), Jung points out that the ego is not only the offspring of the Self but also the parent, and draws the parallel of each of them, ego and Self, to both figures in the biblical "sacrifice" of Isaac by Abraham.
18. von Franz 1966, 17.
19. Jung 1963 and Jung 1969b.
20. Jung 1969b, par. 636.
21. Quoted in Jung 1959, par. 110.

CHAPTER 5: AWAKENING
The epigraphs are from Dickinson 1960, 538, and Patchen 1969, 362.
1. The message of exploitation is found in Genesis 1:28 ("Multiply and . . . subdue [the earth]") and in the expectation of apocalyptic intervention by God (see the next section in this chapter).
2. See 2 Corinthians 5:17.
3. von Franz 1980a, 171.
4. It is a helpful visualization to remember that nature does indeed wait to be discovered. From the rate at which startling new phenomena emerge, we can see the futility of attempting to picture for all future time all that is unknown in the sciences. The sense of nature waking when discovered can be stirred somewhat by remembering the fact that some scientific concepts that interpret nature effectively to us seem to pop up in many places at once when the time is ripe.
5. One Christian, or "post-Christ-

NOTES

ian," who has helped many to rethink this problem is Paul Tillich. His powerful sermon "You Are Accepted," found in *The Shaking of the Foundations* (Tillich 1948, 153–163), already mentioned in chapter 1 above, has been very formative of my present views.
6. In conversation with the author, San Francisco, 1981.
7. von Franz 1980b, 7, 17. This theme also pervades her book *Projection and Recollection* (1980a).
8. Werfel 1976, 595.
9. We must always examine our responses in these experiments for signs of egocentricity.
10. Some branches call this energy *Shakti*.
11. Jung 1967, xxxix.
12. Jung 1969b, par. 579.
13. Ibid., par. 740.
14. Jung 1970, par. 492.

CHAPTER 6: FOSTERING
The epigraph is from Blake 1975, plates 14, 27.
1. Examples of the first way the cosmos serves life include the basic principle of quantum physics known as "complementarity" and its offspring, the "uncertainty principle," along with the "exclusion principle," which gives rise to unique atomic species or elements.
2. The second way the cosmos serves life includes such things as the fact that a proton is 1,836 times as massive as an electron; the fact that the strong nuclear force is 10^{40} times as strong as gravity; and the numerical relationships of the constants of nature, such as Planck's quantum constant of action, along with the speed of light and the electrical constants related to it. A good source of discussions of these things is Weisskopf's *Knowledge and Wonder* (Weisskopf 1979), or my *Atoms, Snowflakes and God* (Hitchcock 1986), as well as Freeman Dyson's *Disturbing the Universe* (Dyson 1979).
3. The distance from Earth to the Sun is about one hundred million miles. Travelling for four years, light would traverse about two hundred thousand times as far as from here to the sun, so that the total distance is the twenty trillion miles just mentioned.
4. Hoyle 1979, 17–21.
5. The sense of a center to space is that every point looks out toward the rest. Our space actually fits the ancient image of the universe whose center is everywhere and whose circumference is nowhere.
6. See note 12 of chapter 1 above.

CHAPTER 7: PHYSICAL GATHERING AND LAYERING
The epigraph is from Moon 1970, 9.
1. In this matter, as in many of the phenomena of the psyche that relate to our worldview, we are left with the nagging question as to whether we discover or invent what we see. Most scientists would argue vehemently that the external world is indeed objective and that it cannot be questioned that we discover the nature of physical reality. On the other hand, one of the most creative physicists of this century, Einstein, said that the laws of

physics are "free inventions of the human intellect" (Einstein 1954, 272). We describe even facts in language that we can never make quite precise when it comes to matters of subtlety. We also do not have such a thing as a philosophical, or absolute, certainty at many points. For example, we do not question whether a certain image really is a car coming down the street that might hurt us if we stepped in front of it. We trust our visual senses in our daily living without debating philosophic issues.

2. This comparison is possible because of the equivalence of matter and energy, established by Einstein in his formula $E = mc^2$, allowing us to quantify both matter and energy in units of density, such as grams per cubic centimeter. The density of energy was many billions of times greater than that of matter.
3. These particles were described in chapter 1.
4. Carl Sagan's *Cosmos*, both in book form (Sagan 1980) and in video form (Sagan and Druyan 1980), shows the evolution of life in its early stages better than any other source of which I know.
5. This level also presupposes a psyche which is stable and proof against mere hallucination, that is, which is not "insane" but is acting upon considered reflection.
6. In order for the process to work without lenses, the light used to make holograms must be of a special sort: the kind that is produced by lasers. The kind of holograms that are sold as knickknacks are actually far more complicated than the type I am describing and do not require the viewer to have laser light to reconstruct their images.
7. Neumann 1989, 9–10.

CHAPTER 8: PSYCHIC GATHERING AND LAYERING
The epigraph for chapter 8 is from von Franz 1980a, 163.
1. Von Franz 1980a.
2. The more the child is permitted to manipulate parents and others, the more the attitude of infantile omnipotence is reinforced, and the harder it is to achieve a good orientation to reality later.
3. Jung 1968, par. 121ff.
4. Jung 1969a, par. 507.
5. von Franz 1980a, 7–8.
6. Ibid., 36.
7. Ibid., 27.
8. Moon 1985, 263. The poem is printed by permission of the Guild for Psychological Studies Publishing House, San Francisco, California.
9. See page 91 above.
10. See note 15 in chapter 1 above.
11. See also von Franz 1980a, 21, on the shadow.
12. Jung 1976, pars. 625–631.
13. The images I have just given are derived from a branch of Jewish Kabbalah developed by Isaac Luria in the sixteenth century: The dots are the divine "sparks" that are gathered in the performance of good deeds. Probably the most accessible book on Luria is Fine 1984.
14. Neumann 1954, 260–261.
15. Mandalas are drawings that represent wholeness as such. The sim-

plest is a circle, but such drawings, which can be quite elaborate, usually manifest a fourfold character as well. The simplest of these is ⊕. This represents the differentiated wholeness of a complete lived life, as distinct from the undifferentiated wholeness of the infant.
16. von Franz 1980a, 171.
17. The seminars are those of the Guild for Psychological Studies, of San Francisco, California.

CHAPTER 9: INTEGRATING
The epigraph to chapter 9 is from Teilhard de Chardin 1969, 23.
1. Heschel 1965, 2–3.
2. Teilhard de Chardin 1969, 58.
3. Teller 1969, 83.
4. While not all individual acts are creative, all creative acts are individual, as in the matter of interpreting the cosmos. "Individualism" is usually a mockery of creative individuality because it is a reaction to the collective, rather than a bringing forth of a person's true heart.
5. The other types of love the Greeks identified are *eros*, attraction, a being drawn towards; *philia*, the feeling between friends and the kind of love expressed in *philosophy*, the love of wisdom; and *thela*, willingness or the will toward some end.
6. Tillich 1955, 10. The story is in Luke 7:36–50.
7. Ibid., 7.
8. Hammarskjöld 1964, 205.
9. Mark 10:27, Matthew 19:26, Luke 18:27.

10. See Prigogine and Stengers 1986, 7–9 and 207–209, specifically. The theme of irreversibility runs throughout the work, however.
11. Of course, the image of the process as a "game" is an artifact of our reverting to a view of God as "out there." Yet even in the inward view, God does take a risk in being "with us" (which is the meaning of one of the names of Christ, *Immanuel*).

CHAPTER 10: HEALING
The epigraph to chapter 10 is from Moon 1985, 89.
1. Mark 8:31–33.
2. Isaiah 53:3–5.
3. Jung 1969b, par. 659.
4. By way of caution, let it be noted once again that rationalism is not the needed ability. Rationalism is just as one-sided as, and decidedly more dangerous than, any other unbalanced pole of human being.
5. Neumann 1989, 99.
6. Neumann 1989, 100.
7. This is the same idea as that of Michael Polanyi's "morphogenetic fields" (Polanyi 1962, 398).

APPENDIX 1: CONTRAST-KNOWLEDGE AND FIELD-KNOWLEDGE
1. Polanyi, 1958, 389.
2. Prigogine and Stengers 1986.
3. Neumann 1989, 97, 98.
4. Polanyi 1962, 395–396.
5. Auden 1946, 117.
6. Neumann 1989, 99.
7. Ibid., 99–100.

References

Auden, W. H. 1965. *Collected Longer Poems*. New York: Random House.
———. 1976. *Collected Poems*. New York: Random House.
Blake, William. 1966. *Blake: Complete Writings*. London: Oxford University Press.
———. 1975. *The Marriage of Heaven and Hell*. London: Oxford University Press.
Boehme, Jakob. 1965. *Mysterium Magnum, or an Exposition of the First Book of Moses called Genesis*. Vol. 1. Translated and with a foreword by John Sparrow, and edited by C.J.B. London: John M. Watkins. Reprint of 1654 edition (Cornhill: M. Simmons/H. Blunden).
Buber, Martin. 1947. *Tales of the Hasidim: Early Masters*. New York: Schocken Books.
Dickinson, Emily. 1960. *The Complete Poems of Emily Dickinson*. Edited by Thomas H. Johnson. Boston: Little, Brown.
Dyson, Freeman. 1979. *Disturbing the Universe*. New York: Harper Colophon Books.
Einstein, Albert. 1954. *Ideas and Opinions*. New York: Bonanza Books.
Fine, Lawrence. 1984. *Safed Spirituality*. In the series *Classics of Western Spirituality*. Mahwah, N.J.: Paulist Press.
Golay, Marcel. 1961. "Confessions of a Communications Engineer." *Analytical Chemistry* 33: 23A–31A.
Hammarskjöld, Dag. 1964. *Markings*. Translated by L. Sjöberg and W. H. Auden. New York: Alfred A. Knopf.
Hawking, Stephen W. 1988. *A Brief History of Time*. New York: Bantam Books.
Heschel, Abraham J. 1965. *Who is Man?* Stanford, Calif.: Stanford University Press.
Hirschfield, Jane, ed. 1994. *Women in Praise of the Sacred: 43 Centuries of Spiritual Poetry by Women*. New York: HarperCollins Publishers.
Hitchcock, John. 1976. "A Comparison of Complementarity in Quantum Physics with Analogous Structures in Kierkegaard's Philosophical Writings, from a Jungian Point of View." Ann Arbor: University Microfilms International. Dissertation 76-9150.
———. 1986. *Atoms, Snowflakes and God: The Convergence of Science and Religion*. Wheaton, Ill.: Theosophical Publishing.
———. 1991. *The Web of the Universe: Jung, the "New Physics," and Human Spirituality*. Mahwah, N.J.: Paulist Press.

REFERENCES

———. 1999. *Healing Our Worldview: The Unity of Science and Religion.* West Chester, Pa.: Swedenborg Foundation.
Hoyle, Fred. 1979. *Cosmogony of the Solar System.* Short Hills, N.J.: Enslow Publishers.
Johnson, Josephine. 1937. *Year's End.* New York. Simon and Schuster.
Jung, C. G. 1959. *Aion.* The Collected Works of C. G. Jung, vol. 9, part II. Princeton, N.J.: Princeton University Press.
———. 1963. *Memories, Dreams, Reflections.* New York: Vintage Press.
———. 1967. Foreword to *The I Ching, or Book of Changes,* translated by Richard Wilhelm and Cary F. Baynes. Bollingen Series, vol. 19. Princeton, N.J.: Princeton University Press.
———. 1968. *The Archetypes and the Collective Unconscious.* The Collected Works of C. G. Jung, vol. 9, part 1. Princeton, N.J.: Princeton University Press.
———. 1969a. *The Structure and Dynamics of the Psyche.* The Collected Works of C. G. Jung, vol. 9, part 1. Princeton, N.J.: Princeton University Press.
———. 1969b. *Psychology and Religion: West and East.* The Collected Works of C. G. Jung, vol. 11. Princeton, N.J.: Princeton University Press.
———. 1971. *Psychological Types.* The Collected Works of C. G. Jung, vol. 6. Princeton, N.J.: Princeton University Press.
———. 1975. *Letters 2: 1951–1961.* Princeton, N.J.: Princeton University Press.
———. 1976. *The Symbolic Life.* The Collected Works of C. G. Jung, vol. 18. Princeton, N.J.: Princeton University Press.
Kazantzakis, Nikos. 1966. *Report to Greco.* New York: Bantam Books.
Kierkegaard, Søren. 1948. *Purity of the Heart is to Will One Thing.* Translated by Douglas V. Steere. New York: Harper and Brothers.
———. 1962. *Philosophical Fragments.* Translated by David Swenson and Howard V. Hong. Princeton, N.J.: Princeton University Press.
Kuhn, Thomas. 1970. *The Structure of Scientific Revolutions.* Chicago: The University of Chicago Press.
Lusseyran, Jacques. 1987. *And There Was Light.* Translated by Elizabeth Cameron. New York. Parabola Books.
Main, C. F., and Peter J. Seng. 1965. *Poems.* Second edition. Belmont, Calif.: Wadsworth Publishing Company.
Mollenkott, Virginia. 1987. *Godding: Human Responsibility and the Bible.* New York: Crossroad.
Moon, Sheila. 1970. *A Magic Dwells.* Middletown, Conn.: Wesleyan University Press.
———. 1985. *Collected Poems: 1972–1985.* Francestown, N.H.: Golden Quill Press.
Murry, J. Middleton. 1930. *God.* New York: Harper Brothers.
Neumann, Erich. 1954. *The Origin and History of Consciousness.* New York: Pantheon Books.
———. 1989. The *Place of Creation.* Princeton, N.J.: Princeton University Press.

REFERENCES

Otto, Rudolf. 1958. *The Idea of the Holy*. New York: Oxford University Press.
Patchen, Kenneth. 1969. *Sleepers Awake*. New York: New Directions.
Polanyi, Michael. 1962. *Personal Knowledge*. Rev. ed. New York: Harper Torchbooks.
Prigogine, Ilya, and Isabelle Stengers. 1986. *Order out of Chaos*. New York: Bantam Books.
Reps, Paul, compiler. N.d. *Zen Flesh, Zen Bones; A Collection of Zen and Pre-Zen Writings*. Garden City, N.Y.: Doubleday.
Rumi. 1990. *Delicious Laughter: Rambunctious Teaching Stories from the Mathnawi*. Versions by Coleman Barks. Athens, Ga.: Maypop Books.
Sagan, Carl. 1980. *Cosmos*. New York: Random House.
Sagan, Carl, and Ann Druyan. 1980. *Cosmos*. Carl Sagan Productions/Cosmos Studios. VHS and DVD format.
Saint-Exupéry, Antoine de. 1943. *The Little Prince*. New York: Harcourt, Brace, and World.
Swedenborg, Emanuel. 1996. *Divine Providence*. 2nd ed. Translated by William Frederic Wunsch. West Chester, Pa.: Swedenborg Foundation.
Teilhard de Chardin, Pierre. 1959. *The Phenomenon of Man*. New York: Harper Torchbooks. Referred to in this book as *The Human Phenomenon*.
――――. 1965. *Hymn of the Universe*. New York: Harper and Row.
――――. 1969. *Human Energy*. New York: Harcourt Brace Jovanovich.
Teller, Edward. 1969. "Neils Bohr and Complementarity." In *Great Men of Physics*. Edited by Marvin Chachere. Los Angeles: Tinnon-Brown.
Tillich, Paul. 1948. *The Shaking of the Foundations*. New York: Charles Scribner's Sons.
――――. 1952. *The Courage to Be*. New Haven, Conn.: Yale University Press.
――――. 1955. "To Whom Much is Forgiven . . ." In *The New Being*. New York: Charles Scribner's Sons.
van der Leeuw, Gerardus. 1963. *Religion in Essence and Manifestation*. New York: Harper Torchbooks.
Verdet, Andrè. 1984. *Chagall's World: Reflections from the Mediterranean*. Garden City, N.Y.: Doubleday.
von Franz, Marie-Louise. 1966. *Puer Aeternus*. New York: Spring Publications.
――――. 1980a. *Projection and Recollection in Jungian Psychology*. La Salle, Ill.: Open Court.
――――. 1980b. *The Psychological Meaning of Redemption Motifs in Fairytales*. Toronto: Inner City Books.
Weinberg, Steven. 1979. *The First Three Minutes*. New York: Bantam Books.
Weisskopf, Victor Frederick. 1979. *Knowledge and Wonder: The Natural World as Man Knows It*. 2nd ed. Cambridge, Mass.: MIT Press.
Werfel, Franz. 1942. *The Song of Bernadette*. Translated by Ludwig Lewisohn. New York: Viking.
――――. 1976. *Star of the Unborn*. Translated by Gustave O. Arit. New York: Bantam Books.

REFERENCES

White, Harvey E. 1931. "Pictorial representations of the electron cloud for hydrogen-like atoms." *Physical Review* 37, 1416–1434.
Williams, Charles. 1949. *Descent into Hell.* London: Faber & Faber.
———. 1958. *The Image of the City and Other Essays.* Oxford: Oxford University Press.

Index

acceptance, 93–94
alivenes, xxiii, 14, 34, 53, 95, 144, 189. See also *living*
Anthropic Principle, 23, 27, 29–30, 66, 161–162, 165
apocalypticism, 88–89, 150
archaic identity (of subject and object), 87, 128, 132, 139–141, 193–195
awakening. See *God* and *cosmos*
Auden, W. H., xv, 63, 190
Augustine, Saint, 174

beauty, 47–67, 150, 166, 185
  dark, 56, 77
  and harsh circumstances, 52
  and meaning, 49, 77
Big Bang, 12, 20, 86, 119, 120, 125, 132, 151
black holes, 113–114
Blake, William, 54, 61, 102,116
Boehme, Jakob, 21
Bohr, Neils, 18,31, 186
Buber, Martin, 49
Buddha, 25, 37, 90, 95, 183

centroversion, 147, 172, 178, 180, 181, 191
choice, 18,19, 82
complementarity, 18, 31, 134, 163–164, 186
Confucius, 25,37, 90, 95, 183
consciousness, 5–6, 11–12, 19, 60, 66, 74–75, 83, 99, 120, 136, 143, 181. See also *unconsciousness*
  and creativity, 38

ego-, 75, 95, 135, 148 (see also knowledge, contrast-)
evolution of, xi, 71, 84, 119, 138 (see also evolution)
consistency, nonrational, 44–46, 165–166, 185
cosmos, universe, 61, 120, 155–156, 171–172, 174–175 (see also evolution)
  aliveness of, 14
  awakening of, 85–101
  depth of, 15, 25. See also *Patterning*
  ecology of, 69, 102–116
  face of, xvii–xviii, 69, 72, ,184
  gentleness in, 115
  integration of, 155–172
  taking inside, 77–78, 130, 145, 184
creation, xi
creativity, 24–46, 59, 165
  hallmarks of, 25, 164

death, survival of, 13–15
  consciousness and, 100
Dickinson, Emily, 47, 85
disequilibrium. See *evolution*
doubt, positive function of, 52, 55–56
duality, wave-particle, 18, 28–34
Dyson, Freeman, 50, 69

ego, 74, 80, 98, 100–101, 120, 135–137, 144–145, 180
  defenses of, 144–145
Einstein, Albert, 38
electrons, 32–34
energy, 64–65, 73, 95, 120, 129, 135, 145, 169–170, 178, 181–184

INDEX

"gathering" as release of, 9, 108, 120, 143, 169, 181
channeling of, 150–151
evolution
  of consciousness, 16–17, 61, 70, 129–131, 135
  impediments to, 22
  of cosmos, 3–23, 120–122, 155, 162, 181
  fundamental disequilibrium, 7–8, 20, 71, 73, 127, 156–157
  of life, 128–130
  purposiveness in, 69–71
  of stars, 7–8, 103–106, 119, 122–125, 131

forgiveness, xxvi, 166–168
freedom, xi, xvi, xxvi, 15, 18, 20, 22, 24, 26, 29–34, 36, 44, 57, 73, 76–77, 89, 162, 181, 185
  and consciousness, 60, 76, 89–90, 136, 164
  as divine experiment, 79
  and love, xvi–xviii, xxvi, 44, 57, 89, 115, 166–167

gathering (process). See also *energy*
  physical, 91, 118–134, 147
  psychic, 10, 119–120, 135–154
God, xi, xii, xxv–xxvi, 22–23, 44, 59, 66, 68, 92–93, 95, 100, 117, 143, 146, 171, 174, 176–177, 179, 185
  aspects of, major, 69–77
  awakening of, 82, 85, 97–98, 119, 179–180
  omniscience of, xii, 21, 72, 73–76
  opposites in, 59, 76, 169, 176 (list)
  unconsciousness of, xiii, 21, 75, 81–82
  latecomer in history of religion, 63
Godding, 68–84, 90, 91, 100–101, 118, 174
Golay, Marcel, 113–114
Golden Rule, 153
gravity, 7, 9, 106, 107–108, 111, 112–114, 115, 120, 122, 157, 177–178

Hammarskjöld, Dag, 169
Hawking, Stephen, 12
Healing 173–185. See also *opposites, specific, wound/healing*
heart, 14, 19, 34, 48, 55, 94
  seeing with, xvii, xix, xvii, xix, xxvii, 3, 19, 27, 84, 86, 95, 102, 115–116, 117, 137, 155
Heidegger, Martin, 189
Heschel, Abraham J., 158
hologram, 132, 148, 178
home, 155–156, 172, 180, 184–185
Howes, Elizabeth Boyden, 43
human (humanity), xi, 5, 37, 59–60, 62

individuality, 37–40, 130–131, 168–169, 170
  God bringing forth, 71–72
  infantile omnipotence, 86
inner/outer. See *opposites, specific*
involution. See *cosmos, taking inside*
irreversibility, 169

Jesus of Nazareth, 5, 25, 37, 79–80, 90, 92, 95, 101, 152, 168, 183
Job, 21, 81–84
Johnson, Josephine, xxvii
Jung, Carl Gustav, xxii, 5, 6, 58, 60, 81–83, 99, 100, 137, 138, 143, 146, 158, 172, 189

Kazantzakis, Nikos, 61
Kierkegaard, Søren, xi, 43
knowledge, xvi, 31, 52, 56, 63
  contrast-, 19, 23, 75, 82–83, 98, 134, 136, 143, 145, 146, 177, 180, 186–192
  field-, 75, 134, 177, 186–192
  self-, 11, 15
Kuhn, Thomas, 35–36

INDEX

layering (process)
  physical, 117–134
  psychic, 135–154
life, 12, 25, 34–35, 71, 103–104, 107, 114, 128, 171
  self-originating, 14–15, 71, 127
living (quality of), xxv, xxvii, 3, 9, 13, 14, 17, 22, 34, 43, 68, 84, 88, 146, 156, 164, 174–175. See also *aliveness*
  problems of. See *love*
love (loving), xv–xvii, xxvi, 21, 84, 102, 152, 166, 167, 173, 181, 185
  fulfillment of, xi, xii, 153–154
  through problems, 21, 71, 89, 101, 118, 157, 185
Lusseyran, Jacques, xxii–xxiv, xxvi, 4, 48

matter. See *reality, physical*
McCarthy, Charlene, 94
metabiology, 41–42
mitochondria, 129
Mollenkott, Virginia, 79
Moon, Sheila, 117, 119, 142, 173
Murry, J. Middleton, 40–42
music, 77

Neumann, Erich, xxii, 20, 23, 134, 147, 172, 180, 187–189, 190–191

obstacles (that force us to reflect), 19–20, 100, 161–162
omniscience. See also *God*
  unconscious, 76
opening, 73, 77, 78, 156
openness, 18, 51–52, 59, 77, 79, 118, 158–161, 184
opposites, 18, 36–37, 58–59 (list), 74–75, 76, 81, 121, 132, 156–157, 161, 169, 175, 176, 178, 180
  complex of, 19, 71
  conflict of, 59, 99, 176
  holding, 75, 77, 81, 91, 101, 143, 156, 157, 162–164

nonrational, 71, 73. See also *complementarity*
specific
  heart/mind, xvi, xix, xxiv–xxv, 27, 29, 59, 118, 165, 170, 178
  inner/outer, 11, 95, 132–134, 137
  spirit/matter, xvi, 4, 15, 23, 30, 31–34, 35, 44, 61,, 102 115, 118, 119, 128, 147, 151, 161–162, 177, 178
  wound/healing, xxiv, 118, 153, 157, 185
opus contra naturam, 137, 150, 183
Otto, Rudolf, 49, 75

Patchen, Kenneth, xxvii, 85
Patterning, 15–18, 72–73, 75, 81, 96, 121, 151. See also *cosmos, face of; person, aspect of; Worldfield*
pawn shop, cosmic, 90–93, 119
planets, formation of, 106–110
play, xxi, xxviii, 64
pluralism, 39
Polanyi, Michael, 187, 189–190
Prigogine, Ilya, 169, 187–188
Prime Inhabitant, xxi, 80, 98. See also *Self*
projection (psychological), 10–11, 36, 87–88, 127, 144
  and recollection, 138–141
psyche, xxii, 6–20, 58, 87, 101, 120, 128, 168, 177–181

reality, physical, nonrational nature of, 27–29, 43–46, 73
responsibility, 46, 60

saving, salvation, 62–63
science, xviii, xxiv, 83, 116, 117, 188
seeing, 5–6, 118
Self (archetype), xxii, 21, 41, 70, 75, 83–84, 97, 116, 128, 135, 136, 143–145, 148–149, 158, 169, 172
shadow, 77, 170
space, bent, 110–113

INDEX

spirit-matter. See *opposites, specific*
spirituality, 34–35
stars. See *evolution*
suffering, 96–97, 101, 175–176, 183
Swedenborg, Emanuel, xi
symbols, 146–150, 151–152, 181–184

Teilhard de Chardin, Pierre, 15, 23, 29–30, 155, 161
Teller, Edward, 163
Thoreau, Henry David, 130
Tillich, Paul, 22, 166
transformation, 9, 1, 73, 78, 86, 101, 152, 183–184

uncertainty principle, 31
unconsciousness (in living), 38, 60, 98, 136, 139–140, 157–158, 164, 175

universe. See also *cosmos*
"fine-tuned" 69

values, 39, 40–43
van der Leeuw, Gerardus, 63
von Franz, Marie-Louise, 78, 80, 91, 94, 135, 138–141, 189

Weinberg, Steven, 12, 49
Werfel, Franz, xxvii, 94
wholeness, xxii, xxv, xxix, 16–17, 41, 156, 175–177. See also *metabiology*.
Worldfield, 18–19, 76. See also *Patterning*
wounding, xxvi, 48, 78, 80,90, 137, 154, 162, 164, 167, 173–174
wound and healing. See *opposites, specific*